ELECHI AMADI

THE CONCUBINE

HEINEMANN

Heinemann is an imprint of Pearson Education Limited, a
company incorporated in England and Wales, having its registered
office at Edinburgh Gate, Harlow, Essex, CM20 2JE.
Registered company number: 872828

www.heinemann.co.uk

Heinemann is a registered trademark of Pearson Education Limited

ISBN: 978 0 435905 56 9

Series Editors:
Chinua Achebe 1962–1990
Adewale Maja-Pearce 1990–94

Series Consultant: Abdullrazak Gurnah 1994–97

Printed and bound by Multivista Global Ltd
08   09   10   20   19   18

The Thunder-god feasts in his grove,
Then naps 'twixt rainbows up above;
But justice suffers here below,
And we know not which way to go.

CHAPTER ONE

Emenike was sure he heard someone cough ahead of him. The forest track was narrow, overgrown and winding. He could not see far ahead. He tightened his grip on his razor-sharp matchet and swung his wine calabash over his shoulder with his left hand. He was not afraid but he did not want to be taken unawares. He knew that surprise can beat even the strongest. He was aware that a venerable old chief had died somewhere. This death was kept as secret as possible. This was because they wanted to give the head-hunters who were now abroad in the forests a chance to capture heads for the great burial. One trapper had seen some of these fellows stalking in the forest and so word had gone round Omokachi that the forests were 'unhealthy'. But of course every man who was a man would go about his business, head-hunters or no.

Emenike rounded a bend and faced Madume, a fellow villager. His arms were folded across his chest and his biceps formed two thick knots. He was biting his lips and his eyebrows met in an angry grimace.

'At last you are here,' he spat out.

'Is that how it is?' Emenike retorted. 'Do your worst.'

Emenike guessed Madume's intentions immediately. They had quarrelled over a piece of land the previous day and many villagers had spoken in favour of Emenike. On the strength of this, Emenike had described Madume as, amongst other things, a dishonest land-grabber. Madume had threatened to beat him up and here he was to fulfil his promise.

Emenike was slight of build but well proportioned, and he ranked as an average wrestler. Madume had a narrow square head (axe-headed according to villagers) and an iroko trunk. Worse still, he had a temper as bad as that of a man with whitlows on his ten fingers.

Emenike's knife showed signs of recent sharpening. There was no question of attacking a fellow villager dangling a sharp knife. Madume thought quickly.

1

'We have had enough of words,' he sneered. 'Let's use our hands too. If you think you are a man put down your matchet.'

'You know of course that I come from a family of braves,' Emenike replied. 'Come on then.' He put down his matchet, his eyes riveted on his opponent.

For long seconds Madume sized up his opponent.

'If you are afraid,' Emenike said, 'get out of my way. I am late for my wine-tapping.'

Madume leaped for a flying tackle. His opponent sank on one knee, collected him on his shoulders and flung him heavily to the ground. Emenike disengaged himself and waited. He would not close in yet. Madume got up and decided to come to grips with his man. For several minutes they pushed each other about treading down bushes like antelopes caught in a rope trap. At last Madume got his two arms under his opponent's armpits and began to push him back at full speed hoping that some undergrowth would entangle his legs and make him fall. It almost happened, but as Emenike was about to fall, he turned slightly sideways, engaged his opponent's left leg with his own right leg and did a rapid half-somersault. Madume was thrown into the air over Emenike's head and landed with a thud on the far side. Emenike leaped after him, sat on his stomach and unleashed several painful jabs to his face. As Madume weakened he decided to stuff his mouth with sand as a final humiliation. But as he stretched out his hand for some earth, Madume heaved his trunk sideways, threw off his opponent and got up.

Emenike's caution deserted him as he gained confidence. He charged at Madume but the latter stooped, carried him shoulder high and dashed him to the ground with elephantine fury. Emenike's side hit the jagged stump of a tree and he lay wriggling weakly. His assailant gave him several hard knocks but realizing that he was putting up little or no resistance left him and fled.

When Emenike came to, he could hardly stand. The pain in his side was terrible. With tremendous determination and will-power he trekked home. His tired look and dishevelled hair covered with wild burr frightened his wife Ihuoma when he entered his compound. She helped him in and whispered fearfully, 'Was it a leopard?'

Emenike waved his hands and slumped onto his bamboo bed. He felt a lump in his throat and coughed. There was blood.

2

Ihuoma raced into her brother-in-law's compound. Nnadi was munching the most enjoyable combination of that time of the year – a cob of maize with pear. But Ihuoma's report took away his appetite and he hurried to Emenike.

Soon, the whole village knew there had been a fight. Madume was relieved when he heard that Emenike was back home. It was true he was in very bad shape himself, but the possibility of killing a man filled him with fear. The cost of the rites of purification was prohibitive and even after that he would still be a branded man. So when people came to ask him about it he maintained a sullen silence. But people knew he had great physical advantages over his opponent and was more likely to win. Indeed as Wodu Wakiri, the village wag, pointed out, Madume's weight alone would be enough to make Emenike groan.

Ihuoma
- as a deity
- can be her own concubine

CHAPTER TWO

Madume, now in his early thirties, was by no means a very successful man. His compound was small with only two houses in it. Indeed he did not care for more houses since thatching them in the rainy season was a job he hated. His wife always complained of a leaking roof and had threatened on one occasion to thatch the house herself, to shame him before the village. When she discovered half a dozen canes in her husband's bedroom she thought differently of the matter.

Madume's yams were few. It was a lucky thing that barns were normally constructed in the farms so that it was not easy to know exactly how many ekwes or columns of yams a man had. Still he had to sell his yams at the waterside market during the harvest season and that gave him away.

Wolu, Madume's only wife, bore him four daughters – a most annoying thing, despite the dowries he knew he would collect when they got married. But who would bear his name when he died? The thought of his elder brother's sons inheriting his houses and lands filled him with dismay. But there was time enough to marry another wife and the problem did not bother him unduly. Moreover, his daughters' marriages would provide him with the money for another wife. Wodu Wakiri had started the opening talks on his first daughter, now fourteen years old. But just now there was no telling whether Wakiri was serious or not. Practical jokes were also his stock in trade. There was one thing which Madume had and that was bulk. He was tall and axe-headed and the old men said he had the best pair of calves in the village. His presence during inter-village negotiations always lent a little extra strength to his village Omokachi. But people in his own village age-group knew he was not particularly strong. He was not a good wrestler (although he danced well to the beat of the drums) and many a young man had licked him.

Madume had one fault most villagers disliked. He was 'big-eyed': that is to say he was never satisfied with his share in anything that was good. He would roar until he had something more

4

than his companions' shares. Consequently he was always quarrelling over land, palm wine trees, plantain trees and other such things. That was how he came to quarrel with Emenike.

But he had other reasons for not liking Emenike. The old men always cited Emenike as the ideal young man. He was good looking and well formed, a favourite with the girls. He was just an average wrestler but had the devil's luck of throwing people in spectacular ways which onlookers remembered long afterwards. He had won the old men's confidence and they always let him run errands that required intelligence and the extensive use of proverbs. Perhaps Madume's hatred for Emenike might not have been so great if only the latter had not snatched Ihuoma from him. Madume had hopes of marrying Ihuoma, then the most desirable girl in Omigwe village. Neither Ihuoma nor her parents had been keen on the match, but Madume overlooked this fact when later Emenike married Ihuoma and blamed him wholly for his loss of the girl he wanted.

It was very easy for him to pick quarrels with Emenike because many events called for a degree of intimacy between the villagers. Take the sharing of meat after a general village hunt. Madume would always argue that Emenike had not been particularly active in the killing of a particular animal and so deserved only a fraction of what the old men actually gave him. But Emenike was not afraid of him. He knew he could hold his own against him any day given a fair chance. But a man's god may be away on a journey on the day of an important fight and that may make all the difference. This was clearly what had happened in the last fight between Madume and Emenike.

*

A day after the fight it was clear that Emenike's condition was serious. He himself had tried to make his brother Nnadi and his other relatives feel that he was almost normal. It galled him to think that he was suffering because of a fight with Madume. He would rather die than admit that. Nevertheless Anyika the medicine man was sent for.

No one quite knew where Anyika had come from. True he said he came from Eluanyim but that was nowhere as far as the villagers were concerned. But by now he had stayed so long in the village that people had ceased to bother about where he had come from. To the villagers, he was just a medicine man and a mediator between them and the spirit world. Towards evening, the medicine man came round to see Emenike who was lying in one of his wife's rooms. A glowing fire had been made at the foot end of his bamboo couch. He was shivering and constantly adjusted his legs to be as close to the fire as possible. His feet were grey with several hours' deposit of ashes. He coughed pathetically.

Ihuoma sat on the couch, her husband's head resting on her lap. Nnadi and other relatives ranged themselves on one side of the room. Emenike's children squatted on the floor, the oldest supporting his chin on his palm and peering anxiously into his father's face. Anyika occupied the most central position. An oil lamp stood on a ledge on the wall. For some time there was a disturbing silence. Then Emenike coughed. As if in answer an owl hard by gave vent to a long, eerie hoot. The sound died in a hair-raising *diminuendo*. The medicine man bowed his head. Nnadi exchanged glances with other members of the family. Clearly all was not well.

Anyika found his voice first.

'Well, Nnadi, you know the procedure,' he said.

'Eh, Anyika,' Nnadi replied and brought out two manillas. He knew that the medicine man could not open his medicine bag without this sum, for it would be an insult to his personal gods and they would render his medicines ineffective.

'Let me have some kola nuts and gin,' Anyika said.

These were brought. Anyika broke the nuts, cut them into pieces and threw them outside. He poured out some gin as libation and muttered as each drop reached the ground:

> 'Gods of the night, take this;
> Gods of the Earth, take this;
> Ojukwu the fair, take this;
> Amadioha, king of the skies
> this is yours;
> And you ancestors, small and
> great, Guardians of this compound,
> take this.'

He hung an amulet over the doorway to bar the way for evil spirits. Then he brought out his divination cowries that made his

6

name resound from the waterside village of Omokachi t [...]
far lands of the Wakanchis, a race of dwarfs, whom onl[...]
knew, or so he claimed.

By the time people had stirred from their 'digestion sleep', that
is, the first deep instalment which ends shortly after midnight,
Anyika was through with his divinations. He administered his
drugs and told them what materials they were to collect for a
sacrifice the next day. He removed his amulet but then changed his
mind and replaced it over the doorway.

'Too many evil spirits about,' he announced.

'That is very kind of you,' Ihuoma said.

The medicine man packed and left. Nnadi and others rose to
leave.

'Sleep well,' Nnadi said.

'I am sure he will sleep well,' Ihuoma replied. By now, Emenike
was dozing.

Ihuoma showed her great devotion to her husband in every way
she could think of. She prepared dish after dish to tempt him. She
brought out a new wrapper, and cushioned his head. The very logs
of wood were specially collected. They were logs of the time-
honoured orepe tree which could glow continuously until the very
last bit had been burnt. This ensured a steady supply of heat and
made constant poking unnecessary. In his fevered brain Emenike
blessed his wife.

At last Ihuoma was ready to go to bed. She roused her husband
gently and whispered:

'Shall I lie on the bed by you or do I spread a mat on the
floor?'

'Lie on the floor,' her husband muttered, 'you may hurt my side.
It palpitates as if it is ripe with pus.'

'I think you are right, my lord,' she said.

The first person to arrive in the morning was Anyika. He had
warned Ihuoma not to open the door to anyone until he came.
There was no knowing who would come with what. But after him,
a steady stream of visitors poured into Emenike's sick room.
Wodu Wakiri the wag was among the early callers.

'I hope you slept well,' he said.

'Eh,' Emenike grunted.

'I wonder what Madume meant by such a crazy fight. I thought
that type of thing was now only for children.'

Emenike wanted to explain that his illness was not necessarily a result of the fight, that in any case he threw Madume twice and gave him a worse beating. But his left side ached cruelly and what with the pain and the cough he could not talk properly. He decided to keep quiet.

'Do not take it to heart, Eme,' Wakiri went on, 'after all, you have always felled him in wrestling matches. Your personal god was not at home; that is how I view it. Everyone knows that Madume can only boast of bulk. Even I can throw him, his axe-head and big belly notwithstanding.'

Ihuoma could not restrain a smile. Wakiri was always amusing people. He made fun of everyone. The curious thing was that he himself had very little to recommend him. He was small; somehow his growth had been retarded. He was knock-kneed and had large eyes. Yet no one made fun of him and he was always welcome wherever he went. Perhaps his trick lay in making fun of himself as much as possible and that left people with nothing else to say. For instance, of his protuberant eyes, he remarked that when the creator was making him he had extra materials for eyes. He pointed out that his knock-kneed legs were best suited for Oduma, a village dance. And he was, in fact, a very good dancer. When at last Wakiri left, Emenike missed him.

The next caller was Nwokekoro, the priest of Amadioha the god of thunder and of the skies. He was a short fat man, old but well preserved and had an easy-going disposition. He never seemed to be bothered about anything. He had no wife and no compound of his own. His small house was in his junior brother's compound. He was getting too old for active farming, so his yams were few and he owned very little property. He was friendly with everyone and was highly respected. His office as high priest of the most powerful god lent him great dignity.

The god of thunder was connected with rain, so Nwokekoro was also the chief rain maker. Everyone in the village knew that he kept a mysterious white smooth stone which, when immersed in water, caused rain to fall even in the dry season. Nwokekoro could also dispel heavy rain-bearing clouds by merely waving a short mystic broom black with age and soot. He derived a fair income during wrestling matches and other such occasions when dry weather was most desirable.

Other rain makers stood in awe of him because he had the direct

8

support of Amadioha. They dared not work in opposition to him. There was the case of Ogonda who tried to rival Nwokekoro. A village had hired Nwokekoro to dispel rain during a wrestling match. Ogonda felt he had been ignored and had tried to make rain. He was struck down on that very day by a thunderbolt while collecting herbs by the wayside. It all went to confirm that a man could not wrestle with a god.

'You have survived the night?' Nwokekoro greeted Emenike in the traditional way. He was a mild stammerer. Wodu Wakiri always said he rumbled like thunder when he spoke – a most irreverent joke, seeing that Nwokekoro was the priest of Amadioha the god of thunder. But Wakiri enjoyed an immunity hard to explain.

'Eh,' Emenike replied.

'Amadioha will protect you, my son.'

'Please, Koko, shall we offer Amadioha a cock?' Ihuoma asked. Koko was the nickname by which the younger generation call Nwokekoro.

'My daughter, that will be on Eke, the usual day for sacrifices. Meanwhile I shall pour libations on your husband's behalf.'

Nwokekoro's visit reassured the couple. It was a fact that if Amadioha insisted on taking a man's life, no medicine man could do anything about it and only a medicine man of great confidence would dare to try.

CHAPTER THREE

As Emenike gradually recovered, Ihuoma's anxiety grew less. The children ceased to talk in whispers and played more freely.

It was an Eke. Ihuoma, her husband and the children were in the reception hall of the compound. Ihuoma was busy roasting maize; Emenike and the children busy eating them. They devoured cob after cob and she could hardly keep the roasting in pace.

'Must a mother starve on behalf of her children?' she asked playfully.

'Well, a good mother should,' her husband replied.

'And a good father should too,' she retorted.

'Take a note that I have taken only two cobs.'

'My lord, you have miscounted.'

'I am sure of my figures.'

'Let's count the cobs around you. One, two, three, four plus the one you have now, that makes five.'

'They are not all mine, you see the children keep pushing their finished cobs this way.'

Emenike laughed mischievously and Ihuoma pouted and smiled at the same time.

'Nwonna,' she said, 'get your father a cup of water.'

'If I drink, I shall not be able to eat more.'

'That is the idea, my lord.'

'Ah, women and tricks!'

Emenike drank and walked slowly to Nnadi's compound.

Ihuoma sat with her children watching the lizards playing on the walls of her house. She was a pretty woman: perhaps that was why she married so early. Her three children looked more like her brothers and sisters. She was young; it was easy to reckon her age. Every farm land was used once in seven years. The piece of land on which her father farmed in the year of her birth was farmed for the fourth time last year. So she was just about twenty-two.

Ihuoma's complexion was that of the ant-hill. Her features were smoothly rounded and looking at her no one could doubt that she was 'enjoying her husband's wealth'. Nothing did a husband greater credit than the well-fed look of his wife. In the first year of her marriage, Ihuoma had been slim and quite a few of her more plumpy mates had remarked that food was being wasted on her. Now she had shamed her critics.

Nnenda, a neighbour's wife, sauntered in.

'Ihuoma,' she greeted.

'Nnenda.' Ihuoma replied.

'I have come to ask you to plait my hair next Eke. I hope you will have the time.'

'I believe I will,' Ihuoma said, 'and maybe you would plait mine as well. My hair is almost like that of a madwoman now.'

'Ah but, Ihuoma, you are not to blame. How could you have the heart to plait your hair when your husband was lying critically ill?'

'Indeed. I am so happy he is better now. I was so afraid he might die,' Ihuoma said.

'God forbid. It would be a terrible blow for Omokachi. Your husband is such a fine man.'

At this compliment Ihuoma smiled. Her husband was a ladies' man and many women adored him. Before Nnenda had married Owhoji she had been a keen admirer of Emenike.

Ihuoma's smiles were disarming. Perhaps the narrow gap in the upper row of her white regular teeth did the trick. At that time a gap in the teeth was fashionable. Any girl who was not favoured with one employed the services of carvers who could create them. Of course accidents occurred now and then: a blood clot could blacken a tooth or the carver's chisel graze the tongue. But the risk was worth it. Ihuoma's gap was natural and other women envied her.

'Let me go and prepare the evening meal,' Nnenda said as she rose to go.

'It is good,' Ihuoma replied, 'I shall do the same.'

As Nnenda walked away. Ihuoma watched her unconsciously. Nnenda's behind was not nearly as full as hers even when she had her beads on, she thought. How lucky she was to possess these physical gifts. She wondered what it was like to be ugly.

'Nwonna, get me a mirror and let me see how bad my hair is.' In truth she wanted to gaze at herself. That she was beautiful she had no doubt, but that did not make her arrogant. She was sympathetic, gentle, and reserved. It was her husband's boast that in

11

their six years of marriage she had never had any serious quarrel with another woman. She was not good at invectives and other women talked much faster than she did. The fact that she would be outdone in a verbal exchange perhaps partly restrained her from coming into open verbal conflict with her neighbours. Gradually she acquired the capacity to bear a neighbour's stinging remarks without a repartee. In this way her prestige among the womenfolk grew until even the most garrulous among them was reluctant to be unpleasant to her. She found herself settling quarrels and offering advice to older women.

'Please go home,' she would say to one of a pair of quarrelling women, 'the veins in your neck are bulging out with much talking. Are you going crazy?' And to the other: 'Why, your baby must be crying at home, stop talking and go and feed her.'

'Ihuoma, I hear you,' says the one, 'but imagine this fool of a woman remarking that I am skinny. She knows very well that I am nursing a baby and that I was ill during pregnancy. Look at her legs, as thin as those of a mosquito.'

'But, Ihuoma,' says the other, 'she abused me first. She says I have cheeks as fat as those of a toad.'

'Why won't you both listen to me? I am sure your husbands have not had their evening meals. Why not go and prepare them? By the way I have come to borrow something from you. Take me home and lend it to me.' She would lead one woman home and so end the storm.

Ihuoma stopped admiring herself in the mirror. She came out of the reception hall into the caressing warmth of the setting sun. She could hear the sound of oduma (a dance employing a xylophone) coming from Omigwe, the next village. Omigwe was very close. The time to get to it was scarcely enough for a meal. So she could hear the individual notes of the oduma and she recognized the particular tune being played. It was the tune to a song recently composed to ridicule a married woman who had misbehaved. The woman had paid the full penalty – a goat and twenty manillas – but Omigwe youths pitilessly perpetuated the incident in a song.

'Chineke! What a faultless oduma beater!' Ihuoma exclaimed. She hummed the tune to the beat of the oduma and started dancing. Unknown to her Emenike, who was just coming back, stood at the entrance to the compound watching her. She clutched the free end of her wrapper with one hand and her waist vibrated

12

rapidly. Her first two children Nwonna and Azubuike followed suit.

'Ha, so you dance so well, my children,' Ihuoma said laughing and embracing them.

'Why not?' her husband suddenly cut in. 'They all take after me!'

'So you have been watching us,' she said reproachfully.

'Well, I could not do otherwise.'

'Then honour my dancing with a present,' she said laughing.

'I will,' he said. He went into his bedroom and brought out a manilla.

'Now dance,' he said.

She danced less seriously now, her cheeks dimpled with suppressed laughter. Her husband embraced her in the traditional way and gave her the money.

'Thank you, my lord,' she said and made for the kitchen.

CHAPTER FOUR

Omokachi was a small village comprising eleven family groups. Each family group occupied a cluster of compounds and every compound had a path bursting into the main path running across the village. The main path ran east towards Aliji, a village rather bigger than Omokachi, and west towards another village Chiolu.

But the nearest village to Omokachi was Omigwe. Igwe, the founder of Omigwe, was forced to leave Omokachi when one of his babies cut its upper teeth first. This was a terrible omen signifying that Igwe had done something very wrong, though no one seemed to remember exactly the nature of the offence. Some whispered that he went to work on a Great Eke: others that he accidentally killed a vulture, the sacred bird of Ojukwu. Whatever it was, the sacrifices needed for absolution were too involved and costly. Among other things the medicine man had mentioned seven rams. Igwe could not collect these things and to ward off the wrath of the gods the villagers ejected him from the village. But he prospered (some say he performed the sacrifices later) and founded Omigwe.

Only the braves could go as far as Aliji. It was a whole day's journey from Omokachi. The path went through forests and swamps and there was no knowing when and where head-hunters would strike. When there was any message to be relayed to Aliji two strong men ran the errand. Emenike often went on these delegations.

Chiolu was nearer than Aliji. If one set out after breakfast one would be there before the sun struck the top of the head. As the distance was rather short, it was easy to brush the path periodically and each village cleared its own half of the path. Mini Wekwu, a stream with a powerful god, formed the boundary between the two villages. The worship of Mini Wekwu often coincided with the clearing of the path. Worshippers from the two villages would meet and offer their sacrifices jointly. It established goodwill and the god ensured that no evil crossed from one village to the other. For instance, no wizard from Chiolu would dare cross to Om-

14

okachi to make havoc. Mini Wekwu would certainly liquidate him. For another reason Chiolu was often on the lips of Omokachi villagers. As it was situated due west of Omokachi, people often described the setting sun as 'going to Chiolu'. Ihuoma remembered vividly how when she was small her mother used to say to her after a hard day's work on the farm, 'Look at the sun, my child. We must hurry home before it gets to Chiolu.'

•

Next in rank to Amadioha was Ojukwu, who was said to control smallpox. This disease was so dreaded that villagers dared not call it by name. They called it 'the good thing'. A patient was normally isolated and when he died (at times of starvation) no one dared weep. People merely said mildly that 'the good thing' had claimed him. Worship of the god was most intense at the height of an epidemic and several rules were rigidly adhered to. People went early to bed, and at night no one sang, wept or waved a fire brand. It was not uncommon for the god to visit villagers at such times. He normally appeared in the form of a familiar neighbour or a child to ask for one trifle or the other. He could for instance appear in the form of a woman and ask a neighbour for vegetables to make her soup. Refusal might mean catching the disease. So during epidemics people were kinder and quarrelling women observed a compulsory truce.

The vulture was the sacred bird of Ojukwu and if one settled on a man's roof he ran immediately to a medicine man to divine the message from the god. The findings could be anything from a blood-curdling ultimatum to a goodwill message and the sacrifices varied accordingly.

Amadioha enjoyed a greater prestige than Ojukwu because for his vengeance he employed either a thunderbolt or a swift illness. No man was intrepid enough to swear by him when he was guilty.

After an illness it was customary to offer some sacrifices to Amadioha for all his help. So on one Great Eke (the small Eke alternates with the Great Eke every four days) Emenike made ready to go to the Sacred Woods of Amadioha. As it was a day for general worship, several old men carrying their three-legged chairs trooped towards the shrine. Emenike walked among them, carrying a bright-red cock and two fat yams for his offerings. Nwokekoro, white-haired and portly, led the way and the conversation.

'Yams will do well this year,' he said as they passed a small farm.

'I think so too,' one Chima replied.

'The leaves are already darkening,' said Wosu, a tall, stooping, sinewy man.

'It will make up for last year's poor harvest. I scarcely realized one hundred manillas,' Nwokekoro said. Despite his mild stammering he spoke slowly.

'You are talking of one hundred manillas,' Wosu said, 'it was all I could do to feed myself. I never realized a cowrie.'

At this point they arrived at the scene of the fight between Emenike and Madume.

'Hei!' Wosu exclaimed in his high-pitched voice, 'it looks as if a boa-constrictor was struggling with a rope trap here.'

'No,' Nwokekoro replied. 'This is the scene of the fight between Emenike and Madume.'

'Eme, I gather it was a tree-stump that hurt you,' Chima said, turning back to look at Emenike. Emenike grunted indistinctly.

'His gods were simply not at home. I can't see Madume beating Eme,' Wosu said consolingly.

'Remember there may be other sides to the matter,' the priest replied.

'Quite true,' Wosu agreed. 'Still, Madume suffered severe bruises. But for his wife's ceaseless application of hot water he might not have recovered by now.'

'And yet the land in dispute belongs to Emenike,' Chima said. 'Madume's "big eye" may cost him his life eventually. Like the hunter who was never satisfied with antelopes, he might be obliged to carry an elephant home one day and collapse under the weight.'

They talked less and less as they approached the Sacred Woods of Amadioha. Rank trees bordered the dark path. Some climbers were so thick they looked like ordinary trees. At the shrine absolute stillness reigned and it was quite cold as the high majestic roof of thick foliage, like a black rain cloud, cut off the sun completely. Even the wind could only play meekly among the undergrowth.

The shrine was at the foot of a massive silk cotton tree. It was fenced off with a ring of tender palm shoots and their yellow colour blazed like a flame against the dark background. Nwokekoro went into the temple and placed some kola nuts in front of

16

two carved figures clothed in blood and feathers. The floor of the shrine was ringed with earthenware pots each containing manillas, cowries, alligator pepper and feathers of animals many years old. There were skulls of animals on either side of the two carved figures. Emenike, who had never before been so close to the shrine, peered into the darkness and thought that one or two skulls looked human.

When Nwokekoro came out of the shrine, he moved about so casually that one could not help feeling that somehow there was a great understanding between him and the god. He never hurried and yet he dispatched each part of the ceremony with precision. His face was almost expressionless, but there was an incomprehensible look about his eyes. Instead of looking outwards they seemed to be staring inwards into his head. Although he was obviously concentrating very hard, there was no rigidity about his features. Emenike noticed that the old men averted their faces when the priest appeared to glance at any one of them; so he decided to stare back whenever the priest's glance fell on him. His opportunity came before the thought was through his mind. He gazed at the priest and immediately regretted that he had done so, for in the priest's face he read mild reproach, pity, awe, power, wisdom, love, life and – yes, he was sure – death. In a fraction of a second he relived his past life. In turns he felt deep affection for the priest and a desire to embrace him, and nauseating repulsion which made him want to scream with disgust. He felt the cold grip of despair, and the hollow sensation which precedes a great calamity; he felt a sickening nostalgia for an indistinct place he was sure he had never been to.

He regained consciousness with a start.

'Eme, are you dozing?' Chima asked him in whispers. 'You seem to be nodding.'

Emenike could not find his tongue. He was confused beyond words.

After the main rites Nwokekoro built a fire from a glowing orepe brand which one old man had brought along. The cocks were killed according to ancient rites and boiled with the yams. Before any part of the meal was touched, the priest cut off one wing of the chicken and threw it casually to the right side of the temple. The old men were evidently used to this and did not watch his movement. But Emenike stared after the apparently wasted

17

chunk of meat; in a matter of seconds a huge grey serpent crawled out from behind the shrine and began to swallow its share of the feast. It showed no fear and the old men bowed their heads in reverence. Emenike had heard of this snake but its size and fearlessness was much more than he had imagined. With the corner of his eye he saw the bulge formed by the piece of chicken in its neck and watched it slide gradually towards the stomach.

The god having been fed, the men fell on the remains of the feast. The sun was just starting its journey to Chiolu when the worshippers trooped back to the village.

CHAPTER FIVE

A market day later Ihuoma sat in her husband's reception hall staring vacantly ahead. With characteristic forgetfulness, her children romped about. Now and then one came to grab her for protection from a pursuing brother or sister. She let them play because they brought her back to reality. Every other thing seemed unreal and her senses were numb.

In the middle of the compound stood her husband's grave. The fresh red earth contrasted strongly with the surrounding, like a big red boil on a black skin. Little gutters traced their way downwards from the top of the grave.

Was it not just possible her husband would somehow emerge from somewhere, and the whole thing prove to be a bitter joke? Why should that grave hold her husband so securely? Ihuoma's senses digested the fact of her husband's death very slowly. Unconsciously she called him by name several times a day and sometimes actually waited for him to turn up.

Ihuoma was roused from her reveries by a caller. This time it was Wolu, Madume's wife. She entered the hall quietly and greeted.

'Ihuoma.'

'Wolu, you are welcome,' Ihuoma replied.

For some time neither of them talked. Wolu did not know how to begin. She was sure Ihuoma was by now tired of engaging in forced conversations with sympathizing neighbours. But the thought of her husband's rather recent fight with Emenike worried her and although it was clear that Emenike had died of 'lock-chest', careful observers could not help noticing a link between the fight and his subsequent illness and death.

At first Wolu had thought of not calling on Ihuoma at all, but that would be unheard of and in extremely bad taste. What would other women think of her? Besides, she had a secret liking for Ihuoma. Apart from her obvious beauty, her open, frank and gentle nature appealed to her. Why, even after Emenike's fight with her husband, Ihuoma had greeted her each time they met on the way – a thing most women would not do. It was more usual under such conditions for women to sneer at their opposite number and show every indication of dislike.

At last Wolu found her tongue.

'Ihuoma take comfort,' she said.

'Mmm,' Ihuoma replied.

'I know it will take you a long time to get used to it, but you have to try.'

Ihuoma sighed.

'When I think of your children and the farm I feel for you.'

It was quite usual for sympathizers to say things like this but such reminders merely added to Ihuoma's grief and she sobbed. Some callers wept with her, others looked on dry-eyed and methodically enumerated the various inconveniences which she was bound to suffer as a result of her husband's death.

When Ihuoma began to weep Wolu stopped talking. She felt a deep sympathy and two drops stood in her own large eyes.

Ihuoma's first impulse was to tell Wolu to her face that she was shedding the tears of the wicked. Her husband had as good as killed Emenike and here she was playing her part in torturing her. If that was not so, why had she delayed her call for so long?

But her gentle nature prevailed and she stared at Wolu steadily. Reluctantly she admitted to herself that Wolu's tears were genuine. Still her presence was somehow not desirable and she was relieved when she left.

Wolu too felt the relief that comes at the end of an unpleasant duty. She walked home slowly trying to guess what Ihuoma's feelings were about her. It angered her a little to think that she should come in for blame in the matter. She did not encourage her husband to fight. If anything she was always dissuading him from his frequent quarrels.

Just as Wolu left, Ihuoma's mother, Okachi, came in. She eyed Wolu's retreating figure.

'What does that witch want?' she asked.

'She came to sympathize with me.'

'To mock you, you mean.'

'I do not know.'

'They have killed your husband and now they want to laugh at you. Amadioha will kill them one by one.'

Ihuoma wondered whether Amadioha was not blind at least part of the time. But she kept her irreverent thoughts to herself.

'You are crying again?'

'Really I am not, Kaka, but the tears keep coming.'

'Well, you have to stop it, my daughter. Emenike will seek out his murderers and deal with them from the spirit world.'

'Kaka, do you think that that fight caused his death?' Ihuoma asked in an undertone.

'What else caused it?'

'I thought it was "lock-chest".'

'But what brought about the lock-chest?'

'He worked too hard in the rain.'

'Was that the first time he had worked under the rain? No my child, we know what happened to him. Amadioha will kill them one by one.'

Ihuoma pondered for a while, her face downwards. Then the tears rained fast and thick.

'Kaka, what will I do, Oh what will I do? How can I look after a whole compound, young as I am? Is there no way of bringing back my lord? chei! chei! chei!'

'If you will do nothing but cry then I shall get back to Omigwe. For over eight days you have wept unceasingly. If tears could do it, Emenike would be here now. Why not stop?'

Okachi was angry, but not with her daughter. She was angry at whatever was responsible for making her young daughter a widow. She shifted her anger from Madume to herself: if only her daughter had not married Emenike, if only she had stopped the marriage, some other woman would have now been in her daughter's place. But how late everything was.

Okachi was about to rise when she heard the steps of someone approaching. She was not going to let her daughter be tortured unnecessarily, so she sat tight.

Ekwueme entered the reception hall grazing the soles of his feet against the ground with a peculiar sound. It was an expensive habit. He confessed he often ran his soles against sharp points, but he could not help it. Still, his gait was none the worse for it.

He had called on Ihuoma before, immediately after Emenike's death. Then the men were so busy arranging for the burial and its rites that it was not easy to tell who was there and who was not.

'Ihuoma,' he greeted the young woman.

'Ekwe,' she replied.

'I see your eyes are still wet,' he said. 'If tears would help, why, all the women in the village would mingle their tears with yours to save Emenike. You must realize that nothing can be done now and pull yourself together.'

'Do help me talk to her. I am tired of scolding her,' Ihuoma's mother put in.

'But you cannot stop her when you are also crying yourself,' he said.

'But it is a big loss, isn't it?' Okachi asked.

'Quite true. The old men say that death is a bad reaper; it is not always after the ripe fruit.'

'You speak the truth, my child,' Okachi replied.

Ihuoma's eldest child entered the reception hall.

'Aha, how are you Nwonna? Come and greet me,' Ekwueme said, happy to change the conversation.

Nwonna moved towards him and settled shyly on his lap.

'Greet me,' he said again.

'Greet him,' Okachi urged.

Nwonna merely examined his fingers and said nothing.

'Go on, greet him, Nwonna,' Ihuoma persuaded.

'Ekwe,' Nwonna piped out.

'Nwonna,' Ekwueme replied. 'You are growing very rapidly, my child. At this rate you may wrestle inside the arena instead of outside it during the next wrestling season.'

Ihuoma smiled very faintly.

'I think he will be a good wrestler,' she said. 'He always practises with his mates and he throws quite a good number of them.'

'Ah yes,' Ekwueme said, 'Omokachi has never lacked wrestlers. Last year we beat Chiolu so well on their own ground that their young men refused to partake of the farewell feast at the end of it all.'

'As for Omigwe,' he went on, eyeing Okachi, 'all I can say is that they are our wives.'

'Omigwe is doing well for her size,' Okachi replied. 'You must admit we have some very good wrestlers there. Take Ota Achara the champion for instance, he has no match here in Omokachi.'

'Well, you are bound to defend your village. There is a saying that every mother thinks her child is a leopard for strength.'

'But Ota Achara is certainly good,' Ihuoma put in.

'Well, he is,' Ekwueme admitted reluctantly, 'but the trouble with him is that he is fond of employing his charms. It is difficult to know just how good he is without the help of the numerous talismans and amulets he wears.'

'What wrestler does not use charms these days?' Okachi asked. 'Many of you flock to Anyika during the wrestling season.'

'I don't use any charms myself.'

'That is so, but you are more of a singer than a wrestler. During wrestling matches your back is more often than not dusty.' Okachi gave a short laugh.

Ekwueme took it in good part.

'But at least,' he said, 'you will agree that I wrestle fearlessly. I always take up any challenge from any wrestler no matter how big or how well equipped with talismans. Most of the so-called wrestlers turn down twenty offers before they pitch on one foolhardy weakling. Being too choosy over opponents makes wrestling a dull affair. After all a throw is by no means a serious matter. As Wodu Wakiri says, no one can carry you home just because he has thrown you. It all ends in the wrestling arena.'

'As for Wakiri,' Okachi sneered, 'nothing worries him. What he lacks in strength, he makes up in words. Many wrestlers avoid him, simply because of the way he ridicules his opponents afterwards.'

They all laughed. Ihuoma cut herself short. How could she laugh, she thought, with the earth over her husband's grave still fresh.

When Ekwueme rose to go, Ihuoma was surprised to find the evening shadows about twice the length of their owners. Time had flown so fast.

Ekwueme left, brushing the soles of his feet against the ground in his characteristic way.

'Take comfort,' he said. 'Amadioha and Ojukwu know best.'

CHAPTER SIX

Ekwueme strolled home as the sun sank rapidly to Chiolu. Again and again Ihuoma's picture flashed through his mind – rounded, beautiful, dazzling teeth with a bewitching gap, sorrow-laden eyes. It was too bad that such a young girl should languish in protracted widowhood. But, as yet, there was nothing that could be done about it.

Ekwueme's compound opened on to the branch path leading to Omigwe and was the last compound that way. Just before he turned into the path he met Wakiri, the wag.

'Ekwe,' Wakiri greeted.

'Wakiri.'

'Where are you from?'

'I am from Ihuoma's.'

'Ewu-u, poor girl. It is tragic isn't it?'

'Too tragic for words.'

'Ah yes, that reminds me; we have to compose a song in Emenike's honour. Adiele, the oduma beater, was discussing it with me the other day.'

'Yes,' Ekwueme replied, 'we should have a song ready before the full moon when the next oduma dance will be held. Come over to my reception hut this evening and let us try to make a start.'

'It is well,' Wakiri replied, 'remember not to eat any maize when you get back, otherwise you would frighten me with your croaking.'

The two songsters parted. Wakiri was the village soloist. Villagers said he had a voice as clear as the sound of igele, a hollow metal gong. Ekwueme's voice was in the lower range but no less melodious. He sang 'obo-obo' or alto very well and provided a wonderful accompaniment to Wakiri's clear soprano. Wherever there was singing to be done this pair was indispensable.

'You have been long at Ihuoma's,' Ekwueme's mother said on his arrival.

'The scene was so pathetic that I could not tear myself away

24

quickly. Also Ihuoma's mother, Okachi, was there and we had a little argument over wrestling.'

'Is the baby still suffering from colic?' he went on.

'I think he is getting better, Ekwe,' she replied.

'Of course Anyika's drugs do not often fail.'

Ekwueme went inside his mother's bedroom to examine the child.

'He is sleeping calmly now,' he said. 'Cover him up, the mosquitoes have started biting. Get my bath water ready quickly,' he ordered his junior sister, Nkechi.

'Hot or cold, Ekwe?'

'Hot.'

'Shall I put in the anti-fever leaves?'

'No, those are rotting now. I shall gather fresh ones tomorrow.'

Ekwueme whistled while he bathed. His whistling was peculiar and melodious, and only few could do it well. He whistled two parts simultaneously, and it sounded like a duet. Nkechi always listened to it. It captivated her.

Ekwueme was enjoying his yam foo-foo when Wakiri arrived,

'Eat with me,' he invited.

'Thanks, I have had enough.'

'A bachelor like you can never have enough of well-pounded foo-foo. Come on, have some real woman-pounded foo-foo.'

Wakiri drew near and washed his hands. He swallowed two big balls of foo-foo and explored the rich soup for some fish. He got some and began to wash his hands again.

'Are you through?'

'Yes. I only ate because you insisted. I have really had enough.'

'Well, that is your affair. There is no point insisting that one's neighbour has a headache when he stoutly denies it.'

'You are talking too much,' Wakiri said, 'you will have some pepper going the wrong way.'

Supper over, the two friends set about their composition. Emenike's death provided the theme, the tune and the arrangement of the words presented the problem. At first Ekwueme's sister chuckled with restrained laughter as the two friends rambled uncertainly through the scale hunting for a tune. But as the tune grew, she hummed unconsciously with them. The villagers were about to stir from their first sleep when the songsters finally satisfied themselves.

'You relay the tune to Adiele and let him practise beating it.'

Wakiri nodded and rose to go.

'May the day break,' he said.

'May the day break,' Ekwueme replied.

•

One evening, about one month after Emenike's death, an oduma dance was held in the village arena. The night was clear as it had rained heavily the previous day. The moon was full. The shadows of shade trees were almost as sharply defined as on a bright sunny day.

As the older men moved in, the children who had been playing on the arena lessened their shouting and began to cluster around the musical instruments, itching to have a try at them. One of them sat astride a pair of drums and beat out a random, senseless sequence.

'Get out of there, do you hear?' Mmam the drummer rebuked the offender and strode menacingly towards him. The mischief-maker scampered away; Mmam was known to be hot-tempered and took no nonsense from rude children. Wodu Wakiri had remarked that even the drums had more beating from him than was really necessary.

'Instead of fooling around,' Mmam went on, 'go and get two plantain stems for the oduma.'

The youth went off with his mates to collect the trunks.

'Mmam is fond of beating people,' said one.

'Yes,' said another, 'with his crooked fingers that never stretch out.'

'It is just as if his hands were made for beating drums,' said a third.

By the time they returned with two heavy plantain trunks, the arena was alive with people. The young men talked and laughed loudly. The few girls who had come out stood in two little groups looking on.

The oduma consists of twelve unequal and rather flat pieces of wood carefully smoothed. The shortest is as long as a man's arm, the longest about half as long again. They are normally arranged in order of size, starting with the biggest to the left of the chief beater. The chief beater can alter the arrangements at his discretion. The nature of the tune normally dictates the necessary rearrangement.

The chief beater and his assistant sit on mats on both sides of the oduma facing each other. The assistant beater does less work. His accompaniment is usually not complicated, though it varies with the tune. But he must get it right or ruin the whole performance. There are usually two pairs of drums, the male and female, made from the skins of antelopes. A drummer sits astride a pair and sweats out the hot leg-raising rhythm.

The okwo is no less important. It is essentially a hollow tree trunk. The quality of its tone depends on the capacity and depth of its hollow interior. Four types of okwos are necessary in a complete oduma outfit. The igele, a hollow metal gong with a clear metallic sound, is indispensable in the maintenance of a strict tempo. It is in fact an audible metronome.

At last Adiele the chief beater arrived. Wodu Wakiri and his co-singer Ekwueme could be heard in the distance singing a well-known tune. As they came close to the arena, the beater took it up, the okwos tore the air, the drums vibrated under expert hands and the igele beat out the tempo meticulously. The dance had started.

Young men and women moved round the instrumentalists singing in response to the soloists. The wrappers of the men and the married women swept the arena, but the maidens wore theirs up to knee level and also had beads above the calves, at the ankles and around their waists.

For a time they moved round and round swaying to the rhythm in a half-stoop. Suddenly the soloist stopped and the instruments took over completely. No one talked, not even the old men who sat around the arena on their three-legged chairs. This was the time to know the top dancers. Everyone bent low. Faces were as rigid as masks. The men moved their backs and shoulders but the women moved only their waists and every bit of their energy seemed to be concentrated there. The vibrations were extremely rapid. It was admirable how they maintained the rhythm at such high speeds. For several seconds tension was at fever pitch. Then one by one the men straightened out and watched the women admiringly. They danced so well. It was difficult to choose between them. Adiele belaboured the short high-pitched end of his oduma,

Mmam caressed the crazy edge of his female drum with his crooked fingers, and the women nearly sobbed with enthusiasm. At last the deepest okwo beat out a peculiar sequence and the instruments came to a neat and abrupt stop.

And so the night wore on. The old men and women and the younger children went to bed. The rest braced themselves to dance all night. The next day was Eke, the day of rest. There would be plenty of time to sleep.

The song composed in Emenike's honour was sung with unavoidable melancholy. The tune was charming but the words were sad. Even Wakiri's usually clear voice was tremulous as he sang the first stanza:

Do you know that Emenike is dead?
Eh – Eh – Eh,
We fear the big wide world;
Eh – Eh – Eh,
Do not plan for the morrow,
Eh – Eh – Eh.

The instruments took over for only a short time and few people danced.

•

All through the night of the dance Ihuoma lay tossing on her bed. The gentle night breeze brought the oduma music clearly to her. She had no enthusiasm for it now and listened out of sheer habit. When the song in honour of her husband was sung she wept aloud. Her first son Nwonna woke up and cried too. Their tears flowed freely; Okachi had gone back to Omigwe and there was no one to restrain them.

Ihuoma felt she could never bring herself to dance again and her world would never be the same again. Her hair was closely shaven according to tradition; she looked emaciated; her cheek-bones showed and her voice was husky and uncertain; her dress was untidy.

Her weeping over, she lay down again and tried to relive her short life with her late husband. She saw him coming into the compound slowly. He looked sickly; his chest was grey with the medicines rubbed on it. He approached timidly and sat down in the reception hall.

'Where have you been my lord?' Ihuoma asked.

'I have been at Nnadi's,' he replied.

'But I have been looking for you all these days. Are you better now?'

'I believe I am improving. Is the food ready?'

'Yes, my lord, come in and let us eat.'

'No, I prefer to eat here.'

'It is well. I shall go and fetch it.'

Ihuoma ran into the kitchen. To her dismay she discovered that the foo-foo was not ready. She hurried with the preparations but no matter how hard she tried she could not cook fast enough. She decided to carry only the soup to her husband. But he was no longer in the reception hall. She called and called and looked everywhere for him but in vain. Then she started to sob and woke with a start. The dream had been vivid and her eyes were wet with tears when she woke.

CHAPTER SEVEN

A year after Emenike's death, the rains had come again and the farms were blooming. As the leaves of maize changed from deep green to dying yellow, the yam foliage, enjoying more space, darkened in colour. Farmers were reassured and worked with a will.

Ihuoma's farm was in good shape, but it was much smaller than it had been. She had sold off a good proportion of her husband's stocks. A woman was not expected to grow yams as extensively as a man.

Each day when she returned from the farm she brought back as much wood as she could carry. Her first son Nwonna helped. This was to prepare for her husband's second burial rites which had been fixed shortly after the new yam festival. This was particularly convenient because at that time there would be enough yams to feed the great number of people who would attend the ceremony.

Ihuoma was sure many people would attend. Her husband had been a popular young man and his many friends would come to pay him the last respects. The prospects of having to feed many people did not frighten her. She knew it was her duty and that the more efficiently she discharged it the more honour she would accord her departed husband.

For his part, Nnadi, Ihuoma's brother-in-law, concentrated on storing dried meat. Instead of selling animals that fell to his many traps, he cut them into bits and smoked them for storage. This would provide the necessary delicacy for the huge pots of soup that would be prepared during the burial rites.

As for goats and chickens Ihuoma merely had to go behind her house to find what she needed for the ceremony. However, she hoped that the mourners would not demand a very large goat, since that would mean slaughtering the leading breeder in her herd – a big toad-bellied she-goat. Apart from its breeding, Ihuoma had other reasons for not wanting to lose this particular goat. She was a rather intelligent animal and never strayed. Even during the full moon when other goats could not tell night from day and rounding them up was difficult, Ihuoma's goat would trot home at the right time leading her young ones. Still no sacrifice was too great in her last homage to her husband.

'You need not worry,' Nnadi said, 'I shall see that the mourners do not demand anything beyond what tradition lays down.'

'No, I am not worrying, Nnadi,' Ihuoma said, 'but you can be sure I shall spare no pains to bury my lord decently. I am even prepared to pawn my best wrappers; after all now that he is gone, for whom shall I dress? Whose admiration do I care for?'

Nnadi knew that this trend in their conversation would end in tears, so he tried to steer her out of it.

'I have been wondering where to build the booth for the mourners,' he said. 'Where do you suggest?'

'Let it form an extension to the reception hall.'

'That is a good idea. I shall start tomorrow. The guests will begin to arrive on Nkwo market day, which is three days ahead.'

'That is so,' Ihuoma replied. 'By the way, which of our guests are we expecting first?'

'Naturally, the old women. After them, your husband's age-group, then the old men.'

Mgbachi, Nnadi's wife, joined them.

'Ihuoma,' she greeted.

'Mgbachi.'

'My lord, your food is ready. Come and eat before it gets cold.'

'You are fast.'

'Isn't today Eke, the day of rest? Why should I be late in preparing your meals?'

Nnadi thought how lucky he was to have such a dutiful wife. After this second burial, he resolved to buy her a new wrapper.

'We have been discussing Emenike's second burial rites.'

'Indeed. It has not left my mind for many market days now. Ihuoma, we must start intense preparations tomorrow.'

'I agree with you, my sister. I am thankful you are near me. Who can handle a second burial single-handed?'

'Who can indeed. I remember when my father died six, no seven, years ago. My mother and the three other wives nearly collapsed under the strain of the rites.'

On the eve of the ceremony all was ready. Nnadi was putting the finishing touches to the booths whose fresh palm fronds gave a deceptive air of festivity. Ekwueme and Wodu Wakiri were helping him.

'Those old women with long throats are now impatient,' Wakiri reflected, 'I hope they will not arrive tonight.'

Ekwueme and Nnadi laughed.

'That is unheard of,' the former said.

'They have eight good days to stay here,' Nnadi added, 'they needn't hurry.'

Ihuoma came towards the men, her hands grimy with mud.

'Are you working?' she greeted.

'Yes. Ah, you have been plastering the grave?' Ekwueme inquired.

'Yes. It should look neat tomorrow. I thank you both for coming along to help Nnadi.'

'As if we are not doing our duty,' Wakiri retorted. 'Go and cook, woman, and stop bothering us with thanks.'

'I hope you will both have your evening meal here,' Ihouma said.

'I am sure Wakiri will be grateful. He has no wife to cook for him,' Ekwueme replied winking mischievously.

'As if you are fatter than I am!' Wakiri retorted, inflating his small frame comically.

Early the next morning the old women began to troop in. Each carried a small bag neatly folded under her armpit. These bags would later house goat-meat and other delicacies which the women would take back to their children and grandchildren. No mother would go to a feast and fail to bring 'parcels' home to her children, no matter how small her share might be.

To begin with, the old women were welcomed with dried meat in palm-oil sauce.

'We need some more pepper,' said one.

'Preferably fresh pepper,' said another.

Pepper was brought.

'Now the taste has reached the bottom of the stomach,' a tall thin woman declared, her cheeks bulging out.

'Pepper is the very life of this type of sauce.'

'I could vomit without pepper.'

'How else can one warm the stomach?'

'Fresh pepper is particularly suited for dried meat.'

'Dry pepper is just as good if well ground.'

And so the guests chatted, while huge chunks of meat disappeared.

After the midday meal, singing and a faint beating of drums was heard in the distance. One, two, and Emenike's age-group had arrived at the scene clad in war dress, their sharp knives glistening in the sun. They came into the compound with a rush, chanting, panting. Half-way, they paused. The houses shook as they stamped their feet in unison.

Omogu Odulawe
Aye!
Omogu Odulawe
Aye!

Their voices grew louder, their faces wilder. Then they went berserk and in a moment the surrounding bushes were alive with men; strong young men, the stuff of heroes, dancing, jumping, cutting, slashing. Scores of plantain trees fell under their lively matchets. Chickens flew out of their way clucking loudly. Dogs barked, unable to make up their minds whether to run after or away from the frenzied young men. Women and children took shelter knowing full well that they had right of way. As excitement mounted some of the men wept, others gnashed their teeth, others howled wildly. Here was a dance of passion, a dance of anger, a vehement protest against the god of death, an appeal for the recall of their departed comrade.

With a big red cock in either hand, Nnadi finally persuaded the men to reassemble. The cocks were handed over to them along with kola nuts and alligator pepper. Then came gin and palm wine. At night they were served with foo-foo, the two cocks gracing the soup.

Emenike had been a wrestler and no greater honour could be done to him than to stage a mock wrestling match. The drums and other instruments were assembled and all through the night the solid leg-raising beats of the wrestling drums invaded the still night air. The classic throws were demonstrated but everyone took care not to throw anyone else. It was an ill omen to be thrown in a mock wrestling match held in honour of the dead. The next day the old men arrived. They surveyed the havoc done by the young men.

'There is scarcely any plantain standing within sight,' Nwokekoro the chief priest remarked, his eyes wide with disbelief.

'It is almost as if a village elder died,' Chima added.

'Emenike certainly deserves it,' Wosu said.

The old men were served. As they crunched their kola nuts slowly they talked to each other with a dignified buzz, an octave lower than the high-pitched, piping, market-chatter of the women.

Ihuoma did not spare herself. She darted from one group of guests to another seeing that they lacked nothing. Several other women were helping her but somehow she seemed to be every-where. The old men studied her and shook their heads.

'A pity a young woman like this should play this role at her time of life,' Wosu said.

'True. Death is a bad reaper; often plucking the unripe fruit,' Chima replied.

'Poor child, she has lost flesh,' Wosu remarked.

'And laughter too,' Chima added.

'Yes, she is less cheerful. The teeth with the beautiful gap are seldom seen now.'

The ceremony ended after eight days. Ihuoma was now ex-pected to cast off her sackcloth and dress properly, for the first time since her husband's death a year ago. So the next evening, Nnenda her neighbour came to plait her hair.

'Cheil my sister, these eight days have been trying for you,' Nnenda said.

'And for you too,' Ihuoma replied. 'You did just as much work as I did. Take water for instance. Who can count the number of pots of water you fetched?'

This was quite true. Nnenda had worked really hard with a zeal that did her credit. What would she not do for the man she had admired so much and nearly married. But she loved Ihuoma too, like a sister, and the latter was quick to reciprocate this love.

'We shall go to market together tomorrow?' Nnenda asked.

'Yes, we shall.'

'Shall I carry your basket for you? You know you shouldn't carry anything on your first outing.'

'Nwonna will carry my basket.'

'Shall I put the indigo on you? I know I am very bad at making the figures but I shall try.'

'Please do. You do not need to get the figures right. Who is admiring me?'

'Don't say that, Ihuoma. Who in this village does not admire you?'

Nnenda prepared some indigo and traced classic figures on her neighbour's ant-hill-coloured skin.

'You will look beautiful tomorrow,' she said.

'I don't want to look beautiful,' Ihuoma replied.

'Why?'

'Beauty seems to carry sorrow with it.'

'That is not true, Ihuoma.'

'It is. Ugly people do not suffer as much as the beautiful.'

'What about me? I have had my share of troubles and yet I am ...'

'But you are beautiful, Nnenda. Have you forgotten how men fought over you?'

They both laughed.

CHAPTER EIGHT

During her days of mourning Ihuoma wept when she plastered her husband's grave and thought of him as she gathered one item after the other for his second burial. She saddened and sorrowed at the mere look of her sackcloth, but sadness and sorrow go well with loneliness.

With the termination of her days of mourning the pangs of solitude redoubled their sting. It was lucky she had three children and the farm to look after. She threw all her energies into them. Her children were neat and well fed and her farm was so thoroughly weeded that, as Nnenda remarked, one could feed off the ground. But in the evenings, the blank was hard to fill. She developed the habit of going to bed soon after the children had stopped their chatter and dropped off to sleep.

Her long nights' rests soon restored her. She put on a little more weight and her cheeks filled out again. The tired look on her face gave way to a sweet youthful expression, softly alluring, deeply enchanting, which had a bewitching subtlety that only deep sorrow can give. Ihuoma's beauty had returned. Young men and even the old gazed at her again irresistibly.

On some Eke days, Ihuoma went to Omigwe to see her parents. On one particular day, her mother Okachi invited her specifically. She went along with her three children. On arrival they were received by the usual hugs and greetings. Ihuoma's little brothers and sisters enjoyed her visits most. They liked the presents of dried fish and nuts which she invariably brought them, and in addition they enjoyed romping with Nwonna and the other two children.

Ogbuji, Ihuoma's father, received her in his quiet but warm manner. He was a thoughtful man and very handsome. Ihuoma got her beauty largely from him.

'Ihuoma, welcome,' he said.

'Nnanna,' she greeted him.

Nwonna ran to his grandfather to be carried. He was carried and given a long hug.

There are certain critical moments in the preparation of soup when constant attention is vital for a good result. This was what kept Okachi in the kitchen behind the house when Ihuoma arrived. Ihuoma did not wait for her to appear but went to the kitchen with her youngest child.

'Ihuoma, you are looking well, thank God,' her mother said.

'Really? I thought I was losing flesh.'

'No, you are not, my daughter.'

'That is surprising after all this thinking and worrying.'

'What are you worried about?' Okachi queried.

'Nne, I don't know really.'

Okachi narrowed her eyes to slits and looked at her daughter. Then she shook her head imperceptibly. Her daughter averted her eyes. Then quickly she said.

'Let me help you with the vegetables.'

'Go and greet the neighbours first.'

'I shall do that later. I am not going away now.'

Her mother pushed the vegetables towards her and she started arranging them.

'Nne, you look a little tired, have you been ill?' Ihuoma asked.

'No, but like you I have been thinking and worrying.'

'What about?'

'About you, my daughter.'

'But I am all right, Nne. There is no need to worry about me.'

'But you yourself said you have been worrying. What is worrying you is precisely what keeps me awake at night.'

They were both quiet for a time. Ihuoma arranged the vegetables and dexterously cut them into pieces. Then she got some water to wash them.

'You needn't bother,' her mother said, 'I plucked those far above the ground. There is no sand on them.'

Okachi stirred the soup with her ladle and gauged its thickness.

'I shall wait a little longer before adding the vegetables,' she declared.

'Don't make the soup too thick. I prefer rather light soup as you know.'

'I know that only too well, my daughter.'

At last vegetables went in, closely followed by okro and a delicate species of mushroom reputed to taste like chicken. Other condiments followed, in their proper order. An expert knowledge of this order was necessary for real success in soup making, and every mother made sure that her daughter understood it thoroughly. Experience had shown that it was no good putting all the items in at once and letting them boil for the same length of time. Some melted on prolonged heating; others lost their taste or even acquired a positively nauseating taste. On the other hand meat and other items required prolonged boiling to bring out their taste and soften their texture. Timing therefore was most important. At this Okachi excelled and Ihuoma took after her.

'Nne, where did you get this mushroom? It is a long time since I tasted it last. This soup will be really tasty.'

'Chikwe the hunter brought some back from the forest. You will take some back with you.'

'Indeed I must. It is so rare. I wonder why we hardly ever see it at Omokachi.'

'Well, your men don't go far enough into the forest.'

'They do. Ekwueme is a good trapper, for instance.'

'Yes and he is good in many things. He sings so well. I rather like him.'

'I like him too,' Ihuoma said naïvely.

'I am glad to hear that,' her mother replied.

Ihuoma immediately wished she had not said that.

'Why are you glad?' she asked, almost furiously.

'Because he is a reliable young man.'

'His reliability should interest his household only.'

'Well, it interests me.'

Ihuoma stared at her mother in perplexity.

'Look, my daughter,' Okachi said seriously and lowering her tone, 'you need a man to look after you. I don't want you to discourage him.'

Although she had sensed this for some time, Ihuoma was taken aback by the suddenness with which her mother broached the subject. All she could do was to look away and say nothing.

When the soup was done, Ihuoma offered to prepare the foofoo.

'No, the pounding will make you sweat,' Okachi said, 'go and greet the neighbours and let me do it.'

Ihuoma went off to greet her relatives and the neighbours. They congratulated her on the success of her husband's second burial ceremony.

38

'It is not an easy thing for a girl of your age to undertake,' one said.

'You have done well. I am sure Emenike will bless you and keep watch over you from the spirit world.'

Ihuoma came back to her mother's home and the family sat down and ate quietly for a time. Then Nwonna addressed his mother: 'Nne, remember to take some mushroom home.'

'I will, my son,' his mother replied.

'I shall carry it myself,' Nwonna persisted.

'Stop talking, Nwonna,' Ogbuji said, 'you are eating. Ihuoma is this how you are bringing them up?'

'Nnanna, he does not listen to me.'

'Is that true, Nwonna? Then you will come to live with me next year. You will behave like a woman if you are brought up by a woman.'

'As if all women were fools,' Okachi retorted.

'Well, many of you are,' her husband replied.

'My lord, some men are more foolish than women.'

'Keep quiet, woman, and eat!'

'I am sorry, my lord.'

There was another quiet spell.

'Put out some more soup, Nne,' Nwonna piped.

'You seem to be exploring the soup with your five fingers,' Okachi said laughing. 'I don't blame you, the soup is good. What do you say, my lord?'

Ogbuji smiled.

'Are you begging me to praise you?'

'Please praise me or I shall praise myself.'

'Well, the soup is delicious no doubt, but I suspect the fish and meat I provided played a great part. I should share the praise with you.'

'Indeed! Then tomorrow I shall just boil only your fish and meat and see how you like it.'

'That would surely fetch you a beating.'

There was laughter.

'But, father,' Ihuoma said, 'Nne cooks really well.'

'Who ever denied that?' her father asked.

'But you never praise her.'

'There is no need to.'

'How will she know what types of soup please you most?'

'That is easy; from the quantity of foo-foo I consume.'

Ihuoma laughed and started coughing.

'Give her water,' her father said.

'Soup has gone the wrong way,' her mother said. 'That is what you get from letting your father tease you.'

After the meal they chatted for a long time. Then as the sun travelled towards Chiolu and the shadows grew longer than their owners, Ogbuji went off to tap palm wine. The children were tumbling outside on the sand. Okachi and her daughter sat in a room talking in low tones.

'My daughter, do you know why I have called you?' Okachi started.

'No, Nne.'

'Listen then. It is over a year since Emenike your husband died. You have conducted yourself in a way which shows that you sucked my breasts. The period of mourning is over now and you are very young.'

'What do you want me to do, marry again?'

'Not if you don't want to.'

'Then what?'

Okachi stared at her daughter, a little confused.

'Still, you need a man to look after you,' Okachi pressed on.

'Nnadi my brother-in-law is doing it well,' her daughter replied.

Okachi paused again to think.

'But surely you need another man.'

'I don't.'

'Do you understand what I am getting at?'

'If you mean that I should get a lover, then let us discuss something else because I won't.'

'You will ruin your health fretting over your dead husband. I am worried about you, my daughter.'

'I cannot forget him so soon. He died only a year ago. I shall remain in his house and look after his children until they are grown. Then perhaps I may think of other things.'

Okachi tried to persuade her daughter.

'Ekwueme is a well-behaved young man. I think I mentioned him when we were cooking.'

Ihuoma was a little impatient.

'Why all this fuss? I don't think this matter is particularly urgent. Let us not worry about it yet.'

'Let us drop it then, my daughter. But remember my suggestion. Ekwueme would be my choice.'

Now Ihuoma did a rare thing with her mother – she lost her temper.

'Ekwueme, Ekwueme, what type of Ekwueme is this? Please let me alone, mother,' and she burst into tears.

Okachi was distressed and minded to cry too. It was absurd, she thought, that she – an old woman – should still be enjoying the protection and joys of a husband while her daughter, a mere child, was playing the widow.

'Stop crying, Ihuoma. I shall leave this matter entirely to you. But know that I mean well and if ever you think you need advice and comfort, come to me.'

Ihuoma hurried home with her children. She was sad and confused. She thought it was cruel for anyone to remind her of her loneliness. No one had that right, not even her mother.

CHAPTER NINE

Only the roofs of widows may leak during the rains. Ihuoma was quite prepared to accept this fact as another season of rains prepared to set in. For many days dark clouds gathered and dispersed again as if holding daily meetings to decide on when to come down to earth. They chased one another across the skies, the dark grey overtaking and overlapping the smoky-white. At night the sky winked with silent lightning, illuminating in fits and starts the ghostly outlines of plantains and of bats out on a rampage.

But most people moved about confident that it would not rain for the next eight to sixteen days. They knew it would begin to rain only after the clouds had hung darkly over the shrines of Amadioha for several days in succession. Farmers watched for this sign. Still, it was time to see to leaking roofs.

'I shall work on Ihuoma's roofs tomorrow,' Nnadi announced to his wife as he made thatches in his reception hall.

'Please do so, my lord. I can't bear to see her living under a roof which shows the stars at night.'

'As long as I live, my brother's wife will never suffer that.'

'You will need someone to help you, my lord.'

'I shall invite Ekwueme and his friend Wodu Wakiri the wag to help. I am sure Ekwueme would certainly come.'

'I think so too.'

Husband and wife looked at each other with a half smile.

Ihuoma was busy weeding the compound. She wanted to clear the weeds before the rains came.

'The compound is looking very neat indeed,' Nnadi greeted Ihuoma.

'You know that an untidy compound just makes my body itch. You have kept indoors today, are you well?'

'Yes, I have been making thatches. You know the clouds have been gathering over the grove of Amadioha for the past two days.'

'Yes indeed.'

'And so tomorrow I intend to mend your roof.'

'Ah, Nnadi you are so good. It is almost as if Emenike were still alive.'

'You will lack nothing that is in my power to give.'

'I know that too well. You will need a helper. I wish my son Nwonna were big enough to lend a hand.'

'Never mind; I shall get one or two friends to help me.'

'Which means I must prepare some food. You and your friends cannot work on an empty stomach.'

'I shall be all right.'

'Yes of course, but your friends will certainly need some foo-foo and palm wine.'

'I shall bring some palm wine along, you prepare the foo-foo.'

'It is well.'

The next morning, Nnadi and his friends brought heaps of fresh thatches and coils of rope.

'I hope Wakiri will not spend half the time talking,' Ihuoma teased.

'Luckily we do not thatch with our mouths,' Wakiri retorted.

Ihuoma laughed. Ekwueme laughed too but rather absent-mindedly; he was watching Ihuoma keenly.

'Ekwe, how is your mother?' she asked.

'She is well.'

'And the baby? He must be walking now.'

'He is well. He is not walking yet.'

'I must come and see them again. It is almost eight days since I touched that baby.'

Ekwueme's mother's last baby was a wonder to the villagers. Ekwueme was Adaku's first child. Nkechi, Ekwueme's sister, followed over ten years after. After her there were no more children for fifteen years or so. No one dreamt Adaku would have another child and when her belly started swelling again everyone at first, including Adaku herself, thought she was diseased. But Ndalu the expert on childbirth pronounced her pregnant after three months and proceeded to administer potions to her. Excitement grew in the village as the months rolled by. When Adaku put to bed a strong baby son people went wild with joy and surprise. Wigwe, Ekwueme's father called a feast and celebrated for days on end. Women volunteers fetched wood and water and even offered food to the family. The baby boy was thus much pampered: his mother scarcely had need to carry him, as visitors tossed him from one eager hand to another.

Ihuoma went into the house to rearrange the furniture to enable the men to work effectively. This is necessary because one man or more works inside the house while another hands over the thatches on a long bamboo from outside. The bad thatches are removed and replaced one by one.

Nnadi and Wakiri were to work inside while Ekwueme handed over the new thatches to them.

'Ekwe, you will always choose the easy job,' Wakiri said. 'I hoped I would stay outside.'

'I pity you then for being unfortunate,' Ekwueme retorted.

'There is no question of misfortune here. It is a case of long scheming and cool calculations on your part. Ever since we came you have been edging away from the house.'

'Well then, let me trick you for once. Tricks are not meant only for you. You are not a tortoise.'

Nnadi burst out laughing in his rather high-pitched voice.

'I agree with you, Ekwe,' he said. 'Wodu employs tricks in all things except wrestling.'

'You are wrong,' Ekwueme said, 'even there he employs unusual tactics. He tries to keep away opponents by ridiculing them and keeping them laughing all the time.'

'Go on you two,' Wakiri replied; 'today is your day. Ihuoma, please take note of those who are doing the greater part of the talking.'

'I shall be your witness if they accuse you of talking,' Ihuoma said, laughing.

The men worked steadily as they talked and, as the shadows shortened, Nnadi thought of the palm wine he had brought.

'You know I have palm wine?' he said.

'And what have you been waiting for? It is lucky I have not taken any water yet. I nearly asked Ihuoma for some,' Wakiri said.

'No matter how much water you take,' Nnadi teased, 'you will always have space for palm wine.'

'And what about you with your long stomach? What will happen to your share?'

In the reception hall they drank and joked. Later, Wakiri started a familiar tune. Ekwueme supplied the second part while Nnadi joined them hesitantly. Nnadi would rather have listened to the other two than sing himself. But he knew this would not make for

44

good companionship. So he sang on like a man who had eaten maize. At times though, he broke through with a fine, harmonious if accidental tenor part. As the singing warmed Ekwueme looked around for a short drum stick. He found one and, with it, converted one limb of a three-legged chair into a percussion instrument. Inside the kitchen Ihuoma unconsciously ground her pepper to their rhythm and her clear igele voice floated into the reception hall. Wakiri could no longer contain himself. He got up and seizing one edge of his trailing wrapper danced very gracefully either because or in spite of his knock-kneed legs.

One song followed another and the wine gradually disappeared as the shadows began to grow.

Ihuoma served the foo-foo in the reception hall. There was so much fish and meat in the soup that they had to put them on a separate plate, to facilitate the free movement of their balls of foo-foo in the soup.

'Ekwe, your foo-foo balls are as big as the head of a baby,' Wakiri said. 'Every ball leaves a big gap in the plate.'

'If you are about to call for more foo-foo, be frank about it,' Ekwueme replied. 'Ihuoma, please get more foo-foo for Wodu Wakiri the wag.'

'Ihuoma, don't mind him,' Wakiri said quickly.

'I shall get some,' Ihuoma said, 'I have so much left.'

In spite of protests from Wakiri another plate of foo-foo was brought.

'More foo-foo means more soup, Ihuoma,' Wakiri said.

'There goes the man who was protesting,' Ekwueme remarked laughing.

'You called for more foo-foo on my behalf, but you show no signs of washing your hands yet,' Wakiri fired back.

Nnadi shared out the fish and meat as best as he could. It was a tricky business and he had to be careful for the sharer always picked last. So if the shares were unequal he would be obliged to take the least.

'This is good meat,' Wakiri said. 'It is surprising that an antelope should be so nice and tender.'

'You see, it is a female antelope,' Nnadi explained.

'I almost thought it was a porcupine,' Ekwueme said.

'At your age you should be able to distinguish the taste of one animal from another,' Wakiri remarked.

'As if I am not one of the chief trappers of the village,' Ek-wueme said behind a fleshy joint.

'Trapping animals is one thing, distinguishing their tastes a different thing.'

'Well, I leave the tasting to you. You seem to do it well.'

Another short session after the meal brought the thatching to an end. Ihuoma thanked them profusely as she and her children gathered the old thatches for burning.

'I no longer care how heavily it may rain this year,' she said.

'Do not be too sure,' Wakiri replied, 'I have seen the roof of a new house leaking in heavy rains.'

'That shows bad thatching,' Ihuoma said.

'It may also mean that the rains were so heavy that the thatches could not stop them,' Wakiri said.

'From the way you talk, Wakiri, I suspect you have done a bad job,' Nnadi said laughing, as they turned to go.

•

Ihuoma and Nwonna were still busy tidying up the mess the roof repairers had made when Ekwueme returned. Ihuoma looked up and saw him and something ticked inside her. Mastering herself, quickly, she said:

'Did you forget anything?'

'Yes indeed, my matchet,' he replied.

They looked round and found the matchet in a corner of the reception hall. Ekwueme picked it up and stood still, looking intently at Ihuoma.

'Greet Nkechi and the new baby when you get back,' Ihuoma said a little nervously and turned back into the house.

'Ihuoma!'

She turned and faced him.

'I have something important to say to you.'

'Say on.'

'Let us go into your sitting-room.'

'Why not here?'

'Too many sand flies.'

Ihuoma led the way into her sitting-room. Nwonna came and sat beside her. Ekwueme sat opposite, his arms folded across his breast. For a moment he eyed Nwonna and fidgeted uneasily.

'Nwonna, go and warm the soup in the kitchen,' Ihuoma ordered,

'Ihuoma,' Ekwueme began, 'I really don't know how to begin.'

She kept quiet, looking at her well-scrubbed floor. Ekwueme's perplexity grew. He began to trace figures on the floor with the point of his knife.

'You are digging up my floor,' Ihuoma protested.

'You can always scrub it again.'

'I have other things to do.' She did not smile.

There was another pause, a little more uncomfortable than the first. Ekwueme felt that somehow the woman sitting in front of him had suddenly grown a little detached. And yet she was just the same. She did not press him to unburden his mind. She just sat there quiet and contemplative. He played on for an opening.

'I like your ways,' Ekwueme began again.

She said nothing.

'You understand me, don't you?'

Still no answer.

'Ihuoma, are you ignoring me?'

'No, I am listening.'

'But you say nothing.'

'You haven't said much yourself.'

'I have more to say.'

'Go on.'

Ekwueme studied her for a moment. It appeared her mind was far away. But there was no knowing since she looked down and her long eyelashes completely obscured what the lids failed to cover. Ekwueme thought that perhaps sitting beside her might help him make his point. He made up his mind to cross over to her. As he drew in one leg preparatory to rising, Ihuoma raised her head and looked at him fully in the face. He winced, then tried to smile but failed. His attempt to talk ended in a stammer. Clumsily he stretched out his hands to hold her but in his confusion he misjudged the distance and his hands failed to reach her.

'I have boiled the soup, Nne,' Nwonna said, crashing in.

'Let me give the children their evening meal,' his mother said with a half smile, and went into the kitchen behind. Ekwueme was thoroughly mortified. He felt like flogging himself. He must be making a complete fool of himself before this wonderful woman.

It looked as if she would spend an unduly long time in the kitchen and so rather wretchedly he got up and announced:

'I think I will defer this matter till the evening of tomorrow.'

'It is well,' Ihuoma's voice sailed through from the kitchen.

Ekwueme went out and reached the road in a few strides. This woman gave him not the least encouragement, he thought; he went over every detail of their short conversation in his mind and arrived at the conclusion that she did not even like him. At the same time he told himself that this was absurd as she had always received him very amicably – with more friendliness than she had appeared to receive others.

If he found their last talk difficult, the thought of another was unbearable after what he decided amounted to a woeful failure. When he got home, his mother quickly observed that he was not at ease with himself and so kept out of his way. Nkechi his sister prepared his bath, putting in the anti-fever leaves and roots. He did not whistle while bathing. Later Nkechi served his supper.

'This soup is too salt,' he complained.

'It is true,' Nkechi replied. 'I believe I mixed too much salt with the pepper during the grinding. I am sorry. If it is too bad, I shall prepare some yam for you.'

'You should be ashamed to set such stuff before me. You will soon get married. I thought only children made this type of mistake. Here you are, carry your food and eat it all.'

His mother intervened.

'Nkechi almost cried when she discovered that the soup was too salt,' she said.

'And what is the result of her crying? She ought to have prepared another pot of soup instead of crying.'

'Please, my son, bear with us, we shall be more careful next time.'

'I just can't eat this,' he said rising.

Ekwueme was about to go into his room when his father Wigwe came into the compound.

'Ekwe, why was your voice so high?' he asked.

'They poured a manilla worth of salt into the soup. It is terrible.'

'Adaku,' Wigwe turned to his wife, 'did I not say that only I can tolerate that much salt?'

'You did, my lord. But we offered to prepare yams for Ekwe.'

'Ekwe, have some yams, my son,' Wigwe pleaded.

'It is too late. I want to sleep.'

'Sleep then and eat in the morning,' Adaku retorted. 'If your father can take it I don't see why you can't. After all, Nkechi and I are not your wives, I wonder …'

'Oho, I suppose you oversalted the soup deliberately,' Ekwe cut in angrily.

His mother laughed.

'Ekwe my dear, Okorobia, Dimkpa, fine boy, please don't be angry. I shall prepare a wonderful dish first thing in the morning.'

Those endearments were too much for Ekwe. He softened but tried not to show it.

'Who wants to eat early in the morning anyway? That is for women and children.'

With that he strode into his room.

'Adaku,' Wigwe said, 'you must not starve Ekwe this way. In his place I would be angrier.'

'I believe there is something else worrying him though,' his wife replied. 'He wore a sad face when he came in.'

'And what can be his troubles?'

'I don't know. But he was at Ihuoma's today mending her roof with Wakiri the wag and Nnadi.'

'Ihuoma never annoys anyone.'

'Of course not.'

'And Wodu Wakiri is his friend.'

'That is true, my lord.'

'Nnadi is a nice quiet fellow.'

'Quite true.'

'Who annoyed him, then?'

'It may not be deliberate annoyance as such.'

'Well, puzzle it out, Omasirim,' Wigwe said a little impatiently. 'I am going to bed.'

'May the day break.'

'May the day break.'

Ekwueme went to bed feeling wretched. This was his first real encounter with a mature and beautiful woman and he had failed. He was reasonably good looking. He was not a weakling. He was not unduly shy; he could talk to girls fairly easily. Why then did he behave like a carved wooden figure before her? But what was it he really wanted to say to her? This question thrust itself into his mind and he found he could not answer it. Had been irresistibly drawn to her and that was all there was to it.

49

That night she obsessed his dreams filling up every space in the eerie twilight of dreamland. In one particularly vivid dream he was at Ihuoma's house chatting with her when Emenike, Ihuoma's dead husband, strode into the compound.

'Welcome, Eme,' Ekwueme greeted. 'You have stayed away too long. Where have you been?'

'Did I not tell you I was going to farm?' he queried.

'You are working too hard.'

'I am not working at all. I am resting.'

'Why go to the farm to rest? Why not stay with us at home?'

'It is nicer there than here. If you would come along with me you would see what I mean.'

The two friends set out for the farm. Soon they came to a stream.

'We have lost our way; there is no stream across your farm path,' Ekwueme pointed out.

'This is a new path. It is short. Come along,' Emenike urged.

'No, I can't cross. The waters look dark.'

'Come on. See I am almost over.'

'No, I can't cross.'

'Let me come over and help you.'

'No, don't, I am going back.'

'No, you mustn't.'

Suddenly from nowhere other villagers appeared at the scene. Ekwueme had a vague feeling of being familiar with them but somehow he could not see their faces. They all urged him on. When he refused they decided to drag him across. They bore him slowly, ever so slowly, across the stream. But the other shore seemed to recede as they inched their way towards it. With a frantic effort the captive broke loose and raced back. Progress was painfully slow. One villager overtook him and tried to grab him. He screamed and gave a blow. He woke to find his hand aching and his body wet with sweat.

The next morning he told his mother about it.

'Emenike and others tried to drag me across a stream in a dream,' he said.

'Amadioha protect you, my son. We must see Anyika about this. It is no ordinary dream.'

A market day later, Ekwueme was nursing some cuts on his chest into which Anyika had rubbed a potent protective charm. To forget the pain due to these knife cuts, he decided to inspect some near-by traps, in the forest. After sharpening his matchet he set off. Just before he turned off into the forest path he met Wakiri.

'Ekwe.'

'Wakiri.'

'Where are you off to?'

'To the forest to have a look at my traps.'

'You may be lucky today, the rainy season is a good time for trapping.'

'You are right, although one can hardly call you a trapper.'

'You have told me so several times already. Are you never tired of repetition?'

'Wakiri, I must be going. Chatting with you is a full-time job.'

Wakiri laughed. 'It takes two to chat, though,' he said.

'That is not true. You are quite capable of chatting alone. All you need is someone to stand near you.'

'Still, it takes two to chat, even if the listener says nothing.'

'I know what you need. A carved wooden figure to talk to.'

The two friends laughed loud and long, Wakiri holding his hands akimbo to support his heaving shoulders. Then he wiped his tears with the back of his hand and started walking away still laughing. Ekwueme made for the forest track.

The first row of traps yielded nothing. One had caught a partridge, but the bird had escaped leaving a mass of feathers. Two or three had gone off without capturing anything. Ekwueme blamed the tortoise for this. All trappers knew that the tortoise had a way of setting off a trap before going on its way. He walked over to the next row of traps which was as far from the first row as Ihuoma's house was from his. This comparison flashed through his mind as he dodged along through the bush.

The first trap had an antelope in it. It was still alive and struggling. It kicked and jumped frantically when it saw Ekwueme. With two bounds the trapper was beside it. A sharp blow with the blunt edge of the knife and the animal collapsed, blood trickling from its nose.

The trapper set about repairing and resetting his trap. He thought that one of the sticks would not stand the struggles of another animal, so he decided to replace it. He spotted the special trees he wanted and made for them. Later, as he approached his trap the antelope which he had supposed dead disappeared into a

51

clump of bushes with one desperate bound. This was unthinkable. Ekwueme ran after it. It was a race he was to remember long afterwards The animal was considerably weakened and paused momentarily now and then for breath; but still it ran as fast as a man. The trapper stumbled and fell several times. Undergrowths tore his skin and wrapper. He pressed on, hewing a way with his matchet when creepers like barbed wire fenced him in. He observed that each time he stopped the animal also stopped. He hit on a trick. He stopped and pretended to go back but kept the animal under close observation. Then quietly he struck out in another direction, creeping and crawling, towards the antelope.

When he thought he was within striking distance he could no longer see his quarry. Noiselessly it had moved to some cool and shady undergrowth to rest. After much straining and peering, Ekwueme saw it. It was squatting and breathing heavily. He inched his way nearer and then dived towards the animal knife-first. This time he took care to employ the sharp edge of his matchet.

CHAPTER TEN

When Emenike died, Madume's mind was in confusion. His feelings were so mixed that it took him a long time to sort them out.

He never could feel completely free from blame in respect of Emenike's death. The death occurred after he had apparently recovered from the fight but there was no doubt that the fight considerably weakened his resistance against any disease. At first this conclusion plagued his mind and he wondered what retributions the gods had in store for him. As the days went by, however, he grew less worried. He even felt at times that the gods themselves supported Emenike's death. After all, people had fought in the past without being killed and in that particular fight, he had a rougher time than his adversary. It was the tree-stump that had made all the difference. In any case people did not just die without reason. Invariably they died either because they had done something wrong or because they had neglected to minister to the gods or to the spirits of their ancestors.

Emenike's death had less gloomy aspects. For one thing he could now extend his boundary with Emenike indefinitely, or so he thought. He could now pluck the various fruit trees on the land in dispute. He could tap the palm wine trees right inside Emenike's land. Who was there to question him? Nnadi was too reserved to make such noise. As for Ihuoma, he still had to see a woman who vied with a man over the possession of land. However, on second thoughts, he had to admit that Ihuoma enjoyed tremendous goodwill from the whole village. She only had to lodge a complaint and everybody would rally round her.

Ihuoma herself was another pleasant aspect of Emenike's death. Emenike had snatched her from him. Now he had a second chance. But he had his misgivings. Would this woman smile on his advances after the part he had inadvertently played in hastening her husband's death? Women were unpredictable. He remembered when he was courting his wife. She refused to greet him when they met on the village paths and loathed even the very sight of him. He had won her over in the end though not without unduly tough negotiations, with their attendant endless calabashes of wine.

Recalling these amorous experiences of his youth he felt he had several advantages. He had a lot of time. There was proximity. His pair of calves was still the best in the whole village. With confidence he decided to make passes at Ihuoma and to marry her if possible. He reckoned that would clear for all time the land disputes.

'I have not seen Ihuoma for some time now,' he said one day to his wife.

She looked up from the baby she was breastfeeding with mild surprise.

'She keeps to her compound much, but I have been meeting her,' she replied.

'Don't you think she is rather proud?' he asked, more to himself than in conversation.

'I don't think she is. She is just a well-behaved woman who takes good care of herself.'

'Don't you take care of yourself?'

'Has she annoyed you?'

'Not in the least.'

'Then let her alone; she has enough troubles, my lord.'

'You seem to like her very much.'

'I do. She is about the best woman in the village.'

Madume went into the house and fetched a three-legged chair and sat opposite his wife outside.

'Where are the children?' he asked.

'They are playing in the arena,' she said.

He paused for some time, biting one corner of his lower lip.

'Wolu, you will run a little errand for me,' he announced at last.

'Willingly, my lord.'

'You will bear a message to Ihuoma.'

Wolu looked down feeling confused. She did not need to be told. His tone had already given away the nature of the message. She kept quiet.

'You heard me?'

'Yes, my lord.'

'And will you do it?'

'If I can.'

'I am sure you can.'

She was quiet.

'Well, it's just this: I want to begin to be nice to her. If things turn out well, I shall marry her.'

It was just like her husband to think too highly of himself. That was why she had nearly refused to marry him. How on earth did he think Ihuoma could ever consent to marry him?'

'My lord, don't think I am jealous, but I cannot bear your message.'

'Why not?'

'Have you forgotten the fight you had with her dead husband?'

'That is past and done with. I did not kill him, did I?' Unconsciously he lowered his tone.

'You didn't, my lord.'

'Then you will go?'

'Somehow I cannot face her. Why not think of some other woman?'

'Wouldn't you like her to be my second wife?'

'No.'

'Why not?'

'I don't know.'

'Women argue forwards and backwards. A moment ago you said you liked her very much. Now you don't want her to be a part of us.'

'I would gladly be the second wife where she is the first; not the reverse.'

'But you are older than she is.'

'It is true, my lord, but she is . . . she is . . . better than I.'

'In what way?'

Just then the children trooped back, the eldest carrying the youngest on her back.

'The rascals are back,' Madume said.

'All children are rascals,' she replied.

'But I think your children are unusually troublesome.'

'My children. Are they not yours, my lord?'

'They are your children.'

'Are they not yours? Answer me.' With that she picked up her baby and went into the house. She laid the baby carefully on a sleeping mound, went behind the house and wept. As her sobbing grew louder, her husband came to her.

'Just what can you say is wrong with you?' There was no answer.

'An old woman like you ought to be ashamed of crying for no cause.

'Was it because I talked of getting another wife?'

She blew her nose and began to wipe her eyes.

'Look here, some men in my age-group have two wives, others three. I don't see why you want to kill yourself at the mere mention of a second wife.'

'That is not why I am crying, my lord.'

'It is. What else can it be?'·

'It is the way you keep talking of my children as if they are not yours. If they were boys you would regard them more as your children, I am sure. Well, I am not Chineke; I do not create children.'

'Really I was not thinking of that,' Madume reassured his wife.

'You were. It is all connected with your desire to get a second wife.'

'You are certainly not saying that I should not get a second wife or that I don't deserve a baby boy, are you?'

'Amadioha forbid! How can I? Who would be here when in the fullness of time you are seen no longer?'

'Then shut your mouth and stop behaving like a goat.'

Madume got up and strolled not without some heat towards the centre of the village. Half-way there he met Nwokekoro, the priest of Amadioha.

'You stride as if you have had or are about to have a quarrel, Madume.'

'No, Koko, I am hurrying to meet someone.'

'Meet him well, my son.'

They passed each other and walked on. Madume looked ahead and saw Ihuoma carrying a pot of water from her brother-in-law's well. Quickly he tried to banish angry thoughts from his mind and to appear calm. He even managed to force a smile.

'Ihuoma,' he greeted.

'Madume,' she replied and passed on.

'Ihuoma, let me come and help you. There is no one in your compound and I am so near.'

'Don't bother. The pot is not too heavy for me.'

He pretended not to have heard and followed her into the compound. But before he could get to her, she had put the pot down. Embarrassed, Madume turned to go and caught his right foot

56

against the protruding corner of an old hoe half buried in the ground. His big toe nail came off and he cried out in pain.

'What is it?' Ihuoma asked.

'My toe is cut,' he said.

'I am sorry.'

Madume limped to the reception hall and sat down nursing his foot.

'Please let me have some cold water,' he begged.

'Nwonna, get him a cup of water.'

Nwonna brought the cup of water and retired with his mother and the other children to the kitchen behind the house.

Alone in the reception hall Madume sat, feeling confused and wretched. With Ihuoma and her children at the backyard, it looked as if he was alone in the whole compound. He glanced at the centre of the compound and saw Emenike's grave. Then involuntarily he looked down at his bleeding toe. A vague fear came over him and he shivered.

'Nwonna,' he called, but it was only a whisper. There was a lump somewhere in his throat. He cleared his throat noisily and called again. Nwonna came out, took the cup and disappeared into the house. At the same moment Wolu passed by on the road, glanced into the compound hastily and looked away on seeing her husband.

Unnerved and puzzled, Madume retraced his way home. He sat on his three-legged chair biting one corner of his lower lip.

'Fetch me water, Adanna,' he called to his eldest daughter.

'O-o-o dede,' she responded from the kitchen. She ran to him with some water.

'Dede, you are hurt. Chineke! it is a big wound.' She ran back into the house in alarm.

'Nne, dede has cut his toe. Come and have a look.'

'Get back, you two,' Madume snapped. 'My meal ought to be ready now. Wolu, what were you moving about the village for instead of preparing my meal?'

'I went to Ejituru to borrow some vegetables, my lord. I am sorry you hurt yourself. Where did it happen?'

Madume felt completely mortified. He knew his wife was teasing him and in a most annoying way.

'I thought I ordered you back to the kitchen,' he spat out looking up at his wife who was standing in front of him, ladle in hand.

She observed a red hue spreading all over the white of his eyes and obeyed quickly.

•

'You have guessed right,' Anyika the dibia said, 'it is no ordinary injury.' He played and replayed his divination cowries.

'You got the injury at Emenike's.'

'Quite true, Anyika,' Madume agreed.

'You know everything, so there's no point my denying it,' he added after a pause.

'You have even thought of marrying her.'

'Yes, Anyika.'

Anyika cast his cowries to and fro for some time. Then he chewed some alligator pepper and spat it out in a fine spray in front of his temple. Madume watched him keenly, wondering what pronouncements he had up his sleeve. He thought himself clever to have come to Anyika to know the true story behind what he thought of as his toe disaster. He had not been mistaken. The gods were behind it. It was certainly a premonition.

'You were lucky,' Anyika said slowly, 'to have come out alive from Emenike's compound.'

'Ojukwu forbid!' Madume stammered.

'Several spirits swore to kill you there and then.'

'Emenike's spirit must have been among them.'

'No, you are mistaken. He was not among them. Unknown spirits, some of them from the sea, teamed up to destroy you. Let me see, oh yes, Emenike's father was among them.'

'What is their grievance?' Madume queried timidly.

'They don't want you to have anything to do with Ihuoma. They have been on the lookout for you. So far they have been unable to enter your compound because of the talisman you buried at the entrance.'

'What is to be done, dibia?'

'There will be several sacrifices to appease Emenike's father and his train.'

'And you are sure the sacrifices will stop them for all time?' Madume asked with growing trepidation.

'We can only fight the present menace. How can we know what spirits will be seeking after your life in the future? We deal with troubles one by one.'

58

'I ought to trust you, Anyika; you are a great dibia.'

'Trust Chineke who is the creator of spirits and men. Without Him my divinations are void.'

'Let me know the various items involved in the sacrifice.'

'Here they are: seven grains of alligator pepper, seven manillas, an old basket, three cowries, a bunch of unripe palm fruit, two cobs of maize, a small bunch of plantains, some dried fish, two cocks, one of which must be white, seven eggs, some camwood, chalk, a tortoise (or the shell) and a chameleon.'

'Hei, this is a costly sacrifice. Can we not omit a few items?'

'I wish we could, but we dare not. Nothing is more precious than life.'

'I will do my best, dibia. What is the procedure?'

'Listen carefully. First, I shall prepare you a talisman. Into it will go the cowries, alligator pepper, chalk and numerous other items which I will provide myself. The white cock will be killed in front of my temple and its blood and feathers will go to strengthen the talisman which you will wear round your neck hereafter. Secondly we shall fill the old basket with the bunch of unripe palm fruit, plantains, dried fish, two eggs, two cobs of maize, seven manillas and abosi leaves . . .'

'You did not mention abosi leaves at first.'

'It was an omission. Don't interrupt me, please. In the dead of night you will carry the basket and contents to any road junction. You will have to walk fast because spirits will be after the sacrifice.'

'Will you come with me?'

'Of course. Otherwise you would not survive. The basket will be supported on a stick with three forks. The other cock (not the white one) will be strangled and hung from one of the forks of the stick. You will then speak as follows:

'Amadioha, Ojukwu, Mini Wekwu,

Ancestors, Gods of the night!

No one digs up immature yams;

My hair is not grey, my work undone;

Accept my sacrifice and spare me.

'Having said this we shall both run back as fast as possible.'

'With what will I suspend the cock?'

'Any cord will do.'

'How much fish shall I put into the basket?'

'Any quantity you like, but the head of the fish must be there.'

'I have understood. Now let me hear the third sacrifice.'

'This will be performed on the farm road. The tortoise will be killed, if alive, and placed in the middle of the path. Two eggs will be smashed immediately in front of and behind the tortoise. The chameleon will also be killed and its fore and hind limbs tied together in pairs. It will be placed on the back of the tortoise.'

'How does camwood come in?'

'I have left out a few details. Just wait and see.'

'Will I say anything during the sacrifice?'

'No. I shall talk this time.'

'What is the real significance of the third sacrifice?'

'How can you understand, you who see with only two eyes? Roughly the point is this. The tortoise and chameleon walk very slowly, not so?'

'Quite true.'

'And when they are dead they don't walk at all, do they?'

'No.'

'Well, in the same way we shall cripple the spirits pestering you.'

Madume went home feeling reassured. He told his wife about his interview with Anyika but left out the part involving Ihuoma.

'You must begin right now to collect the smaller items.'

'Yes, my lord.'

'I shall take care of the chickens, the tortoise and what else . . . ah yes, the chameleon. I wonder where to get that one. It is very rare.'

'We shall send word to friends in the various villages,' Wolu suggested.

'That is a good idea. Palm cutters stumble on chameleons now and then.'

'A white cock is not easy to get either.'

'It will be easy. I think my mother has one.'

'It is well. I believe we shall assemble the materials earlier than I thought. The sooner the better. To think that evil spirits have been dogging me all these days; it is terrible.'

'It is a blessing that Anyika lives among us, my lord.'

CHAPTER ELEVEN

Nnenda, Ihuoma's neighbour, entered Wigwe's compound feeling a little guilty. She had not been to see Adaku's wonder baby for so many markets. She had no excuse. She had passed the compound on her way to the market and to the dance arena.

'Nnenda, my daughter,' Wigwe exclaimed, 'I have not seen you for some time.'

'Dede, the children have been sickly of late.'

'Poor child. How is Owhoji, your husband?'

'He too has not stirred for three days now. He has a large painful boil on his thigh.'

'Is it ripe with pus?'

'Not yet, dede.'

'Relief will come as soon as the pus is expressed. I must go and see him, even though it is risky for me to do so.'

'Why is that so, a boil is not contagious, is it?'

'It is not, but my body is peculiar. As soon as I see a case of boil, I develop one soon afterwards.'

Adaku who had been bathing came out of the house still rubbing her arms with palm kernel oil.

'I see your eyes at last, Nnenda, my daughter.'

'You must pardon me, Adaku. Please let me carry the baby. How fast he is growing. He will begin to walk any moment now.'

'People say so, but really his growth does not appear remarkable to me,' Adaku said, with pride and tenderness in her eyes.

'No mother ever notices her child's growth.'

The child smiled and beat the air with his arms.

'He smiles like his father. Look at the dimple on the right cheek, so exact.'

Wigwe smiled almost shyly. Then changing the subject:

'Her husband has a boil on the thigh,' he said.

'Ewuuu!' Adaku exclaimed. 'Then I should not blame you for not calling. Is it egbe-ohia?'

'Yes.'

61

'That is terrible. He will be bed-ridden for a market or two. I wonder who shot him in the dream.'

'Where is Nkechi?' Nnenda asked.

'Here she comes,' Adaku said. 'She went to fetch water.'

'Nkechi.'

'Nnenda. How is your husband's boil?'

'It is getting more painful.'

'So you knew Owhoji had a boil and refused to tell us,' Adaku said.

'Nne, I forgot all about it.'

'Nkechi, get us chairs. You don't expect us to stand do you?'

Nkechi fetched two chairs for Nnenda and Adaku. Wigwe left the two women to talk and, as Nnenda rose to go, Ekwueme came home.

'Ekwe.'

'Nnenda.'

'Did you kill any animals today?'

'No. All my traps went off without a single catch.'

'Too bad. Whoever saw you first this morning certainly did not give you luck.'

'That may be true. Let's see, who saw me first this morning?'

'Ekwe,' his mother said, 'don't mention my name because you left so early that I did not see you before you left.'

Ekwueme laughed.

'Nne, you are not the guilty one. You always bring me luck. Actually I don't think I saw anyone before I left this morning.'

'Then you brought about your own bad luck,' Nnenda said teasingly. 'Adaku, I am leaving.'

'Go well, my daughter, and greet your husband.'

'O-oh.'

Somehow Nnenda found herself walking with Ekwueme towards the main road of the village.

'Ekwueme, you looked a little worried,' she said.

'I am not.'

'Why don't you laugh then?'

'It would be crazy to laugh without cause. I have not eaten any laughing mushroom, have I?'

After a pause, Ekwueme went on, 'Nnenda, I have something very important to tell you.'

'What can it be, Ekwe?'

'Can you bear a message for me?'

'Yes, I can,' she replied feeling relieved.

Ekwueme paused, studying the ground.

'Say it Ekwe, I shall help you. Who will be the recipient?'

'Ihuoma.'

They were both silent for a time. Ekwueme's mind suddenly had gone blank and Nnenda was somewhat uneasy. Of course she guessed what the message would be, but she could not predict Ihuoma's reactions. She would probably take it quietly without revealing her feelings. She herself would be only too glad to run an errand like that provided she was absolutely sure Ihuoma would be interested.

'What is the message, Ekwe?'

'Tell her I like her and that I very much want us to be friends, real friends.'

There was a pause.

'Will you relay the message?'

'I shall, Ekwe.'

'When will you bring me word again?'

'On the evening of the brother of tomorrow.'

'Where will I meet you?'

'At the entrance to your compound. You should be there when I shall be passing to fetch water.'

'All right.'

Ekwueme turned round and walked towards his room. His mother had been watching his interview with Nnenda through a kink in the fence round her kitchen. The moody expression on her son's face disturbed her. It was time he got married, she thought, before he ran into trouble.

*

The following day Nnenda fed her children quickly in the morning and went over to Ihuoma's.

'I suppose you will go to the farm this morning?' she asked her friend.

'Yes, I shall.'

'Can we go together?'

'Why ask? As if I wouldn't love to chat with someone along the path.'

'Call me when you are ready.'

'I am ready, get your basket.'

The two friends set out for their farms, which lay along the same path. Indeed nearly all the villagers' farms were strung out along the same winding path. In the middle of the farming season walking along the path was like walking through one very big farm. Ears of maize and wandering yam tendrils caressed passers-by. Everybody knew everyone else's farm and as the two friends walked along they greeted the neighbours without actually seeing them. The mere sound of working implements was sufficient indication of the presence of the owner of any particular farm. This assumption led to a funny mistake. When they were passing by Wosu's farm, Ihuoma greeted:

'Dede, are you working?'

'Yes, my daughter,' answered a shrill voice.

'That does not sound like Wosu's voice,' Nnenda remarked.

'Indeed not,' Ihuoma agreed.

'Who is there?' Nnenda asked.

All was quiet.

'Who is there?' she asked again raising her voice. Then from among the thick yam foliage floated quiet laughter.

'That is Chinwe, Wosu's son,' Nnenda said.

'Chinwe, is that you?' Ihuoma asked.

The boy came forward laughing.

'So you were the rogue calling me your daughter, eh? Your daughter indeed! Where is your father?'

'He is at the far end of the farm.'

The two women moved on. Nnenda cleared her throat. It was the fifth time she had done it.

'Ihuoma, I have a message for you.'

'Really? From whom?'

'From Ekwueme.'

There was silence, during which both friends tried to get into each other's mind.

'Ekwueme wants to be friends with you. He said I should plead for him.'

They walked on for an uncomfortably long time without talking.

'You heard me?'

'Yes, I did.'

Then Ihuoma turned into her farm.

64

'We shall go home together, shan't we?'

'Yes, we shall,' Ihuoma replied.

'Then wait for me.'

Nnenda walked a little farther and branched off into her husband's farm.

At the end of the day's work the villagers went home in small, chatting groups. Owhoji now accompanied his wife and Ihuoma, so confidential talk between the two women was ruled out. Later that evening, after putting the children to bed, Nnenda waited in vain for her husband to stroll out so that she could pay a quick visit to Ihuoma. But Owhoji merely yawned and talked of going to bed. Nnenda could not leave her husband's compound at night merely to chat with a neighbour, so she went to bed wondering what answer to carry back to Ekwueme.

The next day, at the appointed time, Ekwueme strolled aimlessly at the entrance leading to their compound. His arms were folded across his chest, his chin on his chest. Just then his father came towards him.

'Ekwe, shouldn't we cut some branches off this pear tree this year? The compound is too shady.'

'Perhaps we should,' Ekwueme replied, his eyes on the road. How was he to get rid of his father? He dashed back to his room and from its dark interior watched his father. Wigwe studied the pear tree for a surprisingly long time and began to move back into the compound. Half-way, Chima who was passing by hailed him. He moved towards the main road again.

'Wigwe.'

'Chima.'

'How's your baby?'

'He is well.'

'Are your yams doing well?'

'Judging from the greenness of the leaves they are not too bad. But I believe yours are better.'

'You are probably being deceived by the good rows nearest the farm road. The soil there is very good. Farther inside the leaves are a sickly yellow.'

Ekwueme prayed that Nnenda would be late in coming. Otherwise he had no hope of an interview with her. How could he question her in the presence of those two old men, one of them his father?

But the old men talked on and on passing with amazing ease from one topic to another. At last, Ekwueme's patience gave way and he decided to make for the road. Just then Nnenda passed by on her way to the well. If he missed her on the return journey it would be too bad. He moved towards the old men. Chima who was about to take his leave turned round again on seeing him.

'Ekwe.'

'Chichi,' Ekwueme replied calling him by the nickname used by the younger generation.

'I saw you with a porcupine the other day. For how much did you sell it?'

'Three manillas.'

'That was too cheap.'

Ekwueme said nothing more. His silence worked and Chima took his leave. Wigwe began to move back into the compound.

'Ekwe, you seem to be searching for something.'

'Dede, I am waiting for Wodu Wakiri,' he lied quickly. His father went into the house. He saw Nnenda returning, balancing her water pot on her head without holding the pot. This made her stretch her arms sideways, now this arm, now the other. It almost looked as if she was performing a slow dance; she looked so grace-ful. As casually as possible she greeted:

'Ekwe.'

'Nnenda, welcome.'

'Is everyone well?'

'We are all well. How was it? What did she say?' He spoke low.

'She said nothing.'

'Nothing?'

'Nothing. Actually we had very little time for discussion.'

'At least she must have said something.'

'Nothing.'

'You mean she did not like the idea?'

'I can't tell. Wait till I find out more.'

With that she moved on. As a young married woman she knew just how long she could decently converse with a young man.

CHAPTER TWELVE

'Wolu, fetch me water and let me wash my hands,' Madume said panting. The night was as black as soot and the villagers were still in their first sleep.

'Did all go well?' Wolu asked.

'Yes, but it was terrible.'

'How?'

'I could almost feel the presence of the spirits around us. We had to run.'

He washed his hands and wiped his brow with one corner of his wrapper.

'May the day break,' Wolu said.

'May it break,' he replied and went to bed.

Now he was confident that no roving malevolent spirits would disturb him. Anyika was a dibia indeed. He thought of Ihuoma. He wasn't quite so sure he could court her without coming to any harm. He went over in his mind the incident in Emenike's compound when he cut his toe. Clearly Ihuoma would never listen to him. He must give her up if only to spare his life. And the land in dispute? No, he would never give that up. Indeed he felt he should now establish his claim to ownership once and for all.

He woke early and ordered some hot water. Adanna brought him some. With a piece of cloth he kept for that purpose he washed his wounded toe with hot water. The water was very hot. He jabbed at his wound timidly and hissed with pain each time.

'I hope this will not develop into a sore, it looks bad,' he said.

'It is healing?' Adanna asked.

'Fetch me some opolipo leaves instead of talking.'

She ran for the leaves. He crushed some other leaves in his palms and squeezed the juice into his wound. He collected the opolipo leaves from his daughter and covered the wound with them. Then he tied it up with dry white strings from a plantain stem.

'Now the flies will not get at it,' he murmured. He went behind the house and spoke to his wife. 'Wolu, I want to get some plantains for tomorrow's market.'

67

'Please do. We have sold out our dried yams.'

Taking his matchet he went off. He made for the land in dispute which was near Emenike's compound. Looking ahead he observed a plantain tree bend slowly. Someone was obviously harvesting the very bunch he had had his eye on for some time.

'Who is there?' he almost roared as he drew near the spot. There was no reply. The top of the tree disappeared as it bent double. Quickening his pace he reached the tree and saw Ihuoma. The calmness of her features almost unnerved him. Methodically she put the bunch into her basket and lifted it on to her head.

'This is not yours, is it?' Madume asked with a slight nervous ring in his voice which annoyed him.

'I thought the elders had settled this land problem once and for all,' Ihuoma replied, looking straight at him.

'Who told you that?'

'I don't need to be told; I was there.'

'It is not true. Put down the plantain.'

'Why should I? It is mine, it is my husband's.'

'Put it down, I say.' He moved towards her, a nasty smile on his face. Ihuoma put down the basket quietly, removed the plantain and began to move away. Only a very foolish woman would try to struggle with a man. As she turned her back on him, she felt a grip on her arm and she turned to face him, her chest and breast heaving in anger, unable to speak. Her assailant spoke.

'Ihuoma, there really is no need for us to quarrel over a head of plantain, if you will be reasonable. Let's be friends and forget all our disputes. I am tired of them myself.'

With an effort which surprised Madume the woman wrested her arm from his grip and tried to move away. But Madume was quick. He gripped her two shoulders and forced her to face him. Too full for words she looked down and her tears flowed fast.

'Abah! Abah! Death, I have you to blame for this!' she wept bitterly, quietly at first then with a loud wail. Madume let her go and she went home crying.

Nnadi her brother-in-law hurried into her compound.

'What is it, Ihuoma?' he asked breathlessly.

Other neighbours started gathering. Nnenda sobbing in sympathy put her hands around her friend and looked into her face tenderly.

'Ihuoma, what is it? Please tell me,' she pleaded.

68

'It is that wicked fellow, Madume,' she managed to say between sobs.

'Who?' Nnadi roared.

'Madume.'

'Did he touch you?'

'Yes.'

'Did he beat you?'

'He as good as did it.'

'Where is he?'

'He is over there, near those plantains.'

Nnadi raced towards the spot. Other men followed, Ekwueme among them. They reached the scene. Ihuoma's basket was there, the plantain lying close to it. The drooping plantain leaves stirred gently in the morning breeze. Madume had moved farther on examining other plantain trees with affected unconcern. In a moment Nnadi was beside him.

'You big-eyed fool, how dare you touch Ihuoma?'

'If you don't get away fast, your mouth will reject meals today. Why don't you find out the facts before ...' But Nnadi was already on him. The two men closed in, their muscles taking the strain. They heaved and tugged, each wondering what was the best throw to employ in that particular position. But the neighbours moved in and separated them.

'If you think you can chase me out of my land, you are mistaken,' Madume gasped.

'Is this your land, you rogue?' Nnadi fumed.

'You hear that neighbours? He's called me a rogue.'

'I repeat you are a rogue. I would rather die than see you harvest plantains on this piece of land.'

'Just watch, I am going to cut down a head of plantain right now.' With that Madume moved towards a tree with heavy ripe fruits. Nnadi struggled towards him but the neighbours held him fast.

'Don't fight, the elders and priests will decide this matter,' the neighbours said and began to drag Nnadi homewards with great difficulty.

Madume gave a short triumphant laugh and aimed at the middle of a plantain trunk. His matchet sank into the soft stem and the crown of leaves and fruits came bending towards him, covering his head and shoulders. He tried to disengage himself. He was rather late.

'Help! Help, oh help! My eyes! My eyes!' he cried in panic. Surprised and confused the retreating neighbours looked back and stood still for a moment.

'My eyes, my eyes,' Madume cried again, stamping his feet on the ground. With one hand he tried to wipe his eyes, and with the other to beckon to the villagers.

'What is it?' the nearest neighbour asked. The others came round and they examined his eyes.

'Spitting cobra,' someone explained. Instinctively they all looked towards the plantain tree just in time to see the tail of a huge serpent gliding away rapidly.

'Tell us, did the cobra spit into your eyes?' Several neighbours asked almost at once.

'It did.'

They led him home.

'Adanna, go and fetch Anyika,' Wolu ordered her eldest daughter. She ran swiftly to the dibia's hut.

'Anyika, please come quickly,' she panted. 'A cobra spat into my father's eyes.'

'Hold on, child, and let me hold consultations,' he said. He went into his house, faced his temple and stood still for some time. He emerged at last frowning.

'Tell your father that I am too busy to come.'

'But you are doing nothing,' the girl argued.

'Bear my message my daughter and don't argue with Anyika.'

Soon afterwards Wolu herself came to Anyika.

'What is the matter?' she asked.

'Yes, I knew you would come. Now listen. This thing is obviously the act of a god, probably a very powerful god. Before I undertake to treat your husband, I must divine the cause of this trouble and find out whether it is safe for me to come or not.'

Wolu went for some money and came running back. She paid the divination charge of two manillas. The dibia's divination cowries rattled and chased one another on the floor a couple of times.

'Several spirits are involved here,' he said. 'I dare not treat your husband until the gods have been appeased with a suitable sacrifice.'

'What will the sacrifice look like?' the woman asked impatiently.

70

'Let me see. It will involve two rams among other things.' Wolu well-nigh screamed with despair. 'It will take days to get that sacrifice ready,' she said.

'Indeed it will,' the medicine-man agreed.

'Meanwhile, what can you do?'

'Nothing.'

'Nothing?'

'Nothing. You see I have to look after myself too. I cannot afford to offend the gods.'

The woman went back dejectedly. One thing was clear; something had to be done right away, sacrifice or no. She thought of people who could administer eye lotions made from rare herbs. Engrossed in thought she nearly passed her husband's compound. She related her interview with Anyika to her husband.

'Go fetch some eye lotions anywhere,' Madume said desperately, 'my eyes are on fire.'

Neglecting her crying baby she moved off again.

'Come back,' her husband said. She went back.

'Put some milk into my eyes. That may do some good.'

Wolu squeezed some milk from her breast into her husband's red and swollen eyes.

After three days of cool eye lotions and peppery eye drops, Madume's eyes were more swollen than ever. They exuded a yellowish matter which helped to glue the eyelids together. Indeed he had not opened his eyes since the day of the incident.

Meanwhile Wolu was collecting the ingredients for the great sacrifice. Feverishly, laboriously, she bought one item after another. By the end of the fifth day, all was ready. The sacrifice was performed near the sacred groves of Mini Wekwu. By the time Anyika came for the more direct treatment, Madume's pupils were no longer distinguishable from the white part of his eyes. Anyika tried one lotion after another until he had to accept defeat. The hard, cold fact was that Madume was totally blind.

While there was some hope of a cure neighbours called to cheer him. But as he became convinced he would be for ever blind, he refused to see or rather to be seen by callers. He kept to his room and wept like a woman. Wolu sobbed and Adanna and the other children cried. Never had they known such desolation, such misery.

In the two months since Madume's blindness, Wolu had lived

through the most trying period of her life. Her husband was a changed man. She did not blame him. She and her children ministered to his needs with untiring devotion.

The extra attention she had to pay her husband did not bother her so much as the realization that she now had to take some major decisions herself. Looking at their reception hall one day she said:

'I think our reception hall needs repairing,' then added quickly. 'I shall see to it as soon as possible.'

'Leave the reception hall alone,' her husband snapped. 'Who is staying there anyway?'

'It will fall if nothing is done.'

'Let it fall then.'

'Our house is in the same condition,' Wolu pointed out, curious to know what her husband would say.

'What is all this noise about repairing roofs? The dry season is almost here.'

Wolu thought it wise at that point to stop arguing. She would do the repairs without comment. She realized the humiliations her husband suffered over such matters.

'My lord, your meal is ready. Please have it while the soup is hot.'

'What is the hurry? I am not ready to eat just now.'

'It is well, my lord. The younger children will let you have it when you are ready. I am going to the farm with Adanna.'

'Adanna will stay behind to serve me. You can go alone.'

'But there is so much to be done in the farm. Besides I cannot carry back all the cocoyams we want to sell at the next market.'

Madume swallowed hard. 'You are bandying words with me, are you?' The blind man's face twitched with anger. He fingered about for his walking-stick as casually as he could. Wolu instinctively moved back a pace or two. The stick missed her by the length of a finger. A hen foraging with her young ones hard by clucked loudly and puffed out her feathers as the stick whizzed past. The children looked on with fear in their eyes.

An awkward combination of feelings assailed Wolu: she was both angry and sorrowful. She hurried to Chima the chief of the village.

'Please come with some other elders and speak to my husband, otherwise my children and I may not survive another moon.'

72

'Ewu-u! poor child,' Chima said. 'I wonder what we shall do about this.'

Most villagers knew about the constant commotion in Madume's compound and like Chima they felt it was inevitable.

Chima and two other elders sat chatting with Madume towards evening. At last they got to the subject.

'Madume,' Chima said, 'your wife complains that you treat her roughly. We have come to settle your differences.'

'My lords, I have nothing to say.'

'Let's hear your side of the story,' Wosu cut in.

'I say I have nothing to say,' said the blind man.

'Madume, have you no respect for me?'

'I am sorry I don't know who you are,' he lied. 'You see I am blind.'

'Surely you recognize my voice. Why, we have been chatting with you for some time. I am Chima.'

'Well, Chima, if you want me to respect you, go away from here.'

'What have I done? This is the worst form of rudeness I have ever experienced. Are you out of your senses?'

Madume smiled a shallow sickly smile.

'You see I am blind,' he said, the sickly smile still on his face.

'Yes, but you are not crazy.'

'I am worse than a lunatic.'

'Amadioha forbid. You are better than a lunatic, my son.'

Supporting his head with his two hands the blind man gnashed his teeth. The elders went back when Madume declined to say anything further.

'I wonder whether he is not crazy as well as blind,' Webilo remarked as they trooped back.

'Well, he has only himself to blame. I don't see why he should bark at people,' Wosu said.

'The hunter who is never satisfied with small game may be obliged to carry home an elephant one day. I have always said this of him,' Chima said.

'True, the plantain was not his,' Wosu said.

'Of course not. The elders gave their verdict in favour of Emenike long ago.'

If Wolu was uneasy before, she was now panic-stricken. Her husband sat sullenly where the elders left him, his expression ominously blank.

'Wolu, get ready my bath water.' The calmness of his voice frightened his wife.

'Yes, my lord,' she said trembling. She went into the house, making sure that the back door was open all the time. She collected some of her valuable wrappers and made them up into a neat bundle. Then she beckoned quietly to her eldest daughter and whispered to her. Adanna went into the house, discarded her working wrapper and donned a better one. Then she took hold of two of her younger sisters. Her mother carried the youngest in her arms and together they began to creep out of the compound.

'Where are you going, Wolu?' Madume asked suddenly. Wolu and Adanna turned round startled. It took Wolu some time to find her voice.

'I am going to my parents, my lord.'

'Because I am blind?'

'No, my lord.'

'What are your reasons?'

'You are planning to kill me.'

'Come back, Wolu. I shall not hurt you.'

'I must see my parents first.'

'Who will look after me while you are away?'

'I shall be back soon. But my parents must know the situation of things.'

'Don't you pity me?'

'I do. It is your fault that I am going away.'

'When will you come back?'

'Tomorrow morning.'

As soon as the footsteps of the fugitives died in his ears, the blind man groped his way into his house and made the door fast.

*

A dance was to be held in the evening of the next day. On his way to his palm wine tree Adiele, the oduma beater, called on Ekwueme to make arrangements for the evening. It was still early. The mist hung thickly in the air as if to perpetuate the darkness of the night. Adiele sneezed as he inhaled the moist air.

Ekwueme's hunting-bag and knife lay at his feet as he tried to lock his door. The lock was ingenious but simple. It consisted of a long pole in an inclined position, the lower end resting against the foot of the opposite wall and the other end against the door. A stout string tied to the upper end of the pole was passed over the wall into the room.

Carefully Ekwueme manoeuvred the end of the string over the wall and hid it among the thatches.

'Ekwe.'

'Adiele. You are up early. How are your wife and children?'

'They are well.'

'I suppose there is a dance tonight.'

'Yes, Adi,' Ekwueme replied. 'Is that bad drum repaired?'

'No. We want to replace the skin altogether.'

'And have you got a skin?'

'Yes, but it will take some days to dry in the sun. It is fresh, you see.'

'Make sure your dog doesn't get at it.'

'I am no hunter, I keep no dogs.'

'Still, your neighbours own some, no doubt.'

'Quite true.'

'Have you practised the new song?'

'Which?'

'The one about Oji who was pushed down by his wife during a fight?'

'Of course,' said Adiele, laughing.

'You know Oji's wife is quite strong.'

'Yes. No other woman dare face her.'

'One can hardly blame Oji; I am not so sure she would not throw me in a wrestling bout.' The young men laughed and began to move towards the main road of the village.

'By the way, I have decided to drop the other song about Madume and the spitting cobra,' Ekwueme said.

'Oh yes, we can't mock him now that he is blind,' Adiele agreed.

'I have not seen him of late,' Ekwueme said.

'Nor have I. I hear his behaviour has become strange.'

'True. Yesterday his wife ran away when he threatened to beat her savagely.'

'Ewuu! poor Wolu, and who looks after him?'

'I wonder. Perhaps . . .'

'Hold on,' Adiele interrupted, holding up his right hand, 'did you hear that?'

They listened and heard wails muffled by the misty air.

'Who could be beating his wife so early in the morning?' Ekwueme asked.

'Listen again,' Adiele said, 'I think it is worse than that.'

'Yes. Chineke! It sounds as if someone is dead.'

They dashed off in the direction of the now louder lamentations. It was in Madume's compound that people had gathered. The crowd was thicker near the doorway, which looked broken. Wolu was crying hysterically and Madume's younger children cried in sympathy with their mother.

When at last Adiele succeeded in peering into the room, the bulky body of Madume swinging on a noose of his wrapper met his gaze. He drew back in consternation. Some women dragged Wolu and her children into the next compound. The elders sat in Madume's dilapidated reception hall holding a discussion in low tones.

'This is bad, very bad,' Nwokekoro the priest of Amadioha said.

'The question is, who will bring him down?' Chima asked.

'Only a dibia of course. No ordinary man will dare bring him down,' someone explained.

'That is clear even to a child,' Chima said, 'but you see Anyika went to Chiolu yesterday to attend to a sick man. He is not back yet.'

'We have to wait for him. Suicide is so abominable that we cannot do otherwise,' Wosu said, shrugging.

Late that afternoon Anyika arrived back in the village. Armed with amulets and powerful charms, he cut down the body. He fortified two strangers, who were to bear the body, against evil spirits. Then began the long trek to Minita the forest into which bodies rejected by the earth were thrown.

CHAPTER THIRTEEN

One Eke day, Ihuoma sat in her reception hall cracking palm nuts on a heavy log cut for the purpose. The depressions on the busy end of the log spoke of long usage. She looked up and saw Wolu, passing by, moody, clad in black wrapper.

Unconsciously, Ihuoma stopped her cracking and began to think of Madume's death. Somehow she had been convinced that something bad must be in store for a man who was so 'big-eyed'. It was impossible for the wicked to go unpunished, the everwatchful gods of retribution, Ofo and Ogu, always made sure of that. They were not particularly powerful gods but they reminded stronger gods of those due for punishment. But what a terrible end! She thought her husband's death was incomparably more honourable. Still, it was bad for Omokachi village to lose two young men in two years. At that rate there would be too few left to organize village activities. She began to count the really energetic young men of the village. There was Nnadi, her brother-in-law, Adiele, the oduma beater, Wodu Wakiri the wag, Mmam, the drummer with his crooked fingers, Ekwueme, the soloist ... Ekwueme ... yes Ekwueme. A nice young man ... Suddenly a shadow glided across the face of the log. She looked up.

'Nnenda.'

'Ihuoma. You are working hard. Let me see. Chineke! You have almost filled a basket with kernels.'

'What are you doing?' Ihuoma asked.

'I have just finished scrubbing the floor of my husband's house. I want to have a little rest now.'

'Rest here then and keep me company.'

'I will. Where is Nwonna?'

'He is out playing.'

'He should help with the kernels.'

'He is roaming around with his bows and arrows trying to shoot lizards with other children.'

'Lizards which no one ever eats.' The two women burst out laughing.

'People eat lizards in a way,' Ihuoma said thoughtfully.

'I have never heard of that.'

'And even millipedes,' Ihuoma continued.

'You can't be serious, of course,' Nnenda said, wide-eyed with unbelief.

'Well, listen. Have you ever tasted the drug from Anyika's famous udu, that small earthen jug?'

'Is that the drug he administers to people when they swallow poison?'

'Yes.'

'No, I have never tasted it.'

'The ingredients include lizards, millipedes and even toads.'

'Hei! I should vomit if I took it,' Nnenda said, grimacing in disgust.

'And that is exactly what the drug is supposed to do.'

'I hope I will never take it.'

'Don't get poisoned then.'

'I won't, I have no enemies. I am friendly with everyone.'

'Mind what you say,' Ihuoma warned smiling impishly. 'Your husband may overhear you.'

'He should know I don't mean that type of friendship.'

'Still, he may not know what type you mean.'

'Oh, Ihuoma, you are funny,' Nnenda said, laughing.

The pause in their chatter was filled by the sound of Ihuoma's hammer on the palm nuts: Pia, pia, pia, it went.

'Chei!' Ihuoma suddenly cried, rubbing her temple.

'What is wrong?' Nnenda asked with concern.

'A shell from a nut hit me.'

'Ewuu! I am sorry.'

'I am lucky it missed my eye.'

'Indeed.'

Ihuoma rubbed her temple a little more.

'It has caused a little swelling,' Nnenda said, peering into her friend's face.

'Well, let it swell. After all, I have no one to admire me.'

'You don't know what you say. What man in Omokachi does not admire you? Look at Ekwueme, for instance, dying of you.'

'That reminds me, what were you telling me about him?'

Nnenda was pleased at this unexpected opportunity.

'Well, what else does a young man say to a pretty young woman?'

'I am not young.'

'I suppose you are older than Chima, the oldest man in the village.'

'I have three children.'

'The number of children does not indicate age. I have two children and yet I am older than you are.'

'By how much?'

'Over a year.'

'Hei! You exaggerate. It is not more than six months.'

'It is just because we are women. What of the men who are older than we are and who have no children? For instance Ekwueme is older than you are by at least two years if not three.'

'I wonder how you got to know . . .'

Ihuoma checked herself as she heard voices on the path leading to the compound.

'That must be Wakiri the wag and Ekwueme,' Nnenda said, without looking.

'I believe you're right, Nnenda. It is surprising how people turn up when you are talking about them.'

'That is true.'

The two friends reached the reception hall and exchanged greetings with the women. Ekwueme tried to pick up the trend of his conversation with Wakiri. To hide his shyness and gain confidence, he spoke loudly, laughing rather expansively. As the women could not join them it became increasingly awkward and he stopped trying. Wakiri turned to Ihuoma.

'Ihuoma, are your yams dry enough to be tied into ekwes?'

'Yes, they are? Why do you ask?'

'Nnadi has asked me to help him tie them up for you.'

'Oh, thank you.'

'I am not over-interested in thanks. The point is you must make sure you prepare excellent meals.'

'Wakiri, you eat too much for your size,' Nnenda said mischievously.

'Much of the food goes to swell my eyes.' They roared with laughter. Wakiri remained unmoved, blinking his large eyes comically. Nnenda rose to go, her eyes streaming with tears of laughter. She wished Ekwueme had come alone.

When Nnenda left, the flow of conversation died down a little. While Ihuoma was concentrating on her kernels Ekwueme gave his friend a knowing look. Soon afterwards Wodu Wakiri rose to go.

'But you have only just come,' Ihuoma protested.

'Just be sure of the food, that is my point in coming.' He walked away, his knock-knees brushing each other.

Ihuoma knew that the departure of Nnenda and Wakiri was a calculated move and she felt a little embarrassed.

An awkward silence set in. Then Ekwueme had an inspiration.

'Ihuoma, I would like to help tie up your yams.'

'Oh, but the yams are few; a woman's yams always are.'

'Still, many hands make light work.'

'You may speak to Nnadi about it. He is making all the arrangements.'

'I will do so, but will it displease you if I come?'

'How you speak! Why should it displease me?'

'Because you are a woman very difficult to understand.'

'I think I am straightforward.'

'Yes, I know, but you are difficult none the less.'

'You are the one becoming difficult now. I can't quite get at your meaning.'

Here was the chance at last to say something useful. Ekwueme swallowed hard, coughed, cleared his throat, coughed again and swallowed.

Pia, pia, pia, Ihuoma's stone hammer cracked away. It did not quite make up for the silence. Each stroke now sounded hollow and emphasized the silence.

Ekwueme heard himself saying:

'We have composed a new song.'

'Really? How does it go?'

'It is about Oji whose wife Aleruchi threw him down during a fight.'

'Yes, I heard Wakiri talking about it,' she said laughing. 'How does it go?'

Ekwueme cleared his throat.

> 'Aleruchi Oji,
> She is a Champion wrestler
> A mighty leg twist
> Sent her husband down.
> Aleruchi Oji,
> She is a Champion wrestler.'[1]

'It is good. How does Aleruchi take it?'

'We have not sung it openly yet, but there is nothing she or her husband can do about it so long as we are telling the truth.'

'When will it be sung in the arena?'

'Madume's death prevented us from dancing two markets ago. We shall sing it at the very next dance. I hope you will come.'

'Yes, I will.'

'Of course you should. You are one of our best dancers.'

'When I was young, not now.'

'You talk nonsense.'

'I speak the truth. Many maidens dance much better than I do.'

'I tell you, you may be chosen to dance in the Cloth House this year.'

'Do you think any Cloth House will be set up in the arena this year?' Ihuoma asked.

'Why not? What can stop such a strong tradition?'

'Madume's death.'

'But his death is abominable. There will be no mourning, no second burial.'

'That is true.'

Ihuoma heard her youngest child crying in the house. She had just awakened from sleep. She ran to the house, opened the door and carried her to the reception hall. With the edge of her wrapper she wiped the baby's sweating face and fondled her, calling her by many pet names.

'Stop crying, please,' she said. The child continued sobbing. 'What do you want, beautiful one? Fish?' The baby nodded. The mother carried her into the kitchen and gave her a generous portion of dried fish. The child thrust one end of it into her mouth and promptly stopped crying.

'Ihuoma, I have to go,' Ekwueme said, yawning.

'Why not stay a little longer?' Ihuoma said, engrossed with nursing her baby. Ekwueme knew she was merely being polite, and rose to go.

'Will you crack palm nuts tomorrow?' he asked.

'Yes, will you help me?' She was teasing him.

'I am just about too old for that,' he said smiling. He yawned again and stretched himself, clasping his two hands and raising them above his head.

'Don't swallow me,' Ihuoma said, 'you are opening your mouth too wide.' Ekwueme smiled and turned to go. His feet grazed the ground in his characteristic way. He was conscious of Ihuoma's eyes on him as he walked away. He looked back. Ihuoma was caressing her baby, apparently not looking at him at all.

When he got home he threw himself on his bamboo bed and sighed. He thought of Ihuoma. Once again he had failed to un-burden his mind to this woman. Still he cherished every moment spent with her. There was no doubt she was warming to him. Or was she? No, she was just the same; kind, polite, lovable. But staying with her was pleasant and restful. He would be content with that for the present.

The next day, after inspecting his traps, he bathed carefully and gulped down a late breakfast. He tied a clean wrapper and took some time combing his hair. His own comb proved inadequate today and he went to borrow his mother's.

'You have a comb, haven't you?' Adaku asked.

'My hair is getting too long for my small comb.'

The woman took a second look at her son.

'Where are you going?'

'Just strolling out.'

'Why not repair my kitchen? One of the supporting sticks is rotten and needs replacing.'

'I shall get a forked stick tomorrow when I go to inspect my traps.'

'You can do it now. You have nothing to do.'

'I have just returned from the forest. Do you mean I should go back again to hunt for sticks?'

'You needn't go far, my son,' she pleaded.

'But what is the hurry? Tomorrow is almost here,' he said irritably.

'As you wish, my son,' the woman said.

Ekwueme strolled off. His mother's eyes followed him. He was aware of this, so on reaching the main road he turned right instead of left. He walked up to Wakiri's compound. To his relief his friend was not in.

'Ekwe,' the children who were playing in the sand greeted him.

'Are you playing?' he replied.

He turned back. On reaching the entrance of his compound he

82

walked faster. He glanced into the compound and met his mother's gaze. She had come out to spread a wet mat in the sun. Her baby had soiled it the night before. Ekwueme walked past, annoyed for no real reason. When he got to the entrance to Ihuoma's compound he found no one about. He glanced at the reception hall and guessed that Ihuoma was busy on her palm nuts. But he might be wrong and he felt it would not be quite proper for him to walk into an empty compound for no good reason. He moved along wondering how far he should walk before turning round again.

Suddenly he grew ashamed of wandering about aimlessly and turned round resolutely to go home. But as he passed by Ihuoma's compound again he saw her in the reception hall working at her kernels. His feet steered him towards her.

The shells flew this way and that as Ihuoma worked her hammer. Her youngest child was sleeping on a mat beside her. The other child had caught some grasshoppers and was feeding them limb by limb to some ants. He watched with undivided attention, the ants dragging their comparatively mighty burdens into the dark mysterious interior of their holes. Nwonna the eldest child had gone off with his bows and arrows.

The eaves of the reception hall were so low that Ihuoma could only see Ekwueme's knees and ankles as he approached.

'Ihuoma.'

'Ekwe,' she replied looking up and smiling politely. The tiny gap in the white teeth showed. Somehow this gap always lent a subtle shyness to her smile.

'How many baskets have you filled today?'

'One. The children gave me no peace. Where are you from?'

'From my house.'

'I thought I saw you coming from the other direction.'

Ekwueme had to think quickly.

'Oh, I went up there to have a look at something.'

'Any luck with your traps today?'

'None. My trap caught a giant rat but I found only its bones.'

'You must have neglected your traps for some days?'

'No, it was a case of soldier ants.'

'I am sorry.'

'What is bad luck to me is good luck to the ants though.'

'Yes, it is. What hurts one man may benefit another.'

'As I think the parable says, a diseased village is a good village to a medicine man. Am I right? I cannot speak in parables.'

'You don't need to.'

'Why not?'

'You are a woman.'

'Women are unlucky. They are denied many things.'

'List them.'

'They are uncountable. Look, we are not allowed to climb trees, we may not eat the meat of a kite, the gizzard of a bird is also forbidden, we . . .'

'Well, would you like to be a man in your next incarnation?'

'No.'

'There you are!'

They laughed. Ihuoma looked up and their eyes met.

'Are we tying up your yams tomorrow?' Ekwueme asked.

'Yes, if you care to come.'

Ekwueme remembered the promise he had made his mother. He would not fail her. That meant he would have to mend the kitchen right away and have the next day free. He wanted to stay a little longer.

'I wonder how long the shadows are,' he said and went outside. He looked at his shadow and glanced at the sun.

'The shadows are still short,' he said.

'The shadow of your head is like a coconut,' Ihuoma said, smiling broadly.

'With that Ojongo hair-do your shadow should be indescribable,' Ekwueme retorted

'Let's see,' she said giggling. She went out into the sun and they laughed as they measured the shadows.

Now that he was sure of seeing her the next day, Ekwueme decided to go and mend his mother's kitchen.

At home he changed into his hunting wrapper and went into the bush behind their house. He came back with a strong forked stick.

'Ekwe, so you were merely teasing me,' his mother said. Ekwueme smiled, his matchet busy on the stick. He dug a hole near the old rotten stick and drove the new one into it. Then he shifted the weight of that corner of the roof from the old to the new stick.

'Now my ears will enjoy some peace,' he said smiling at his mother.

'It is not as difficult as you tried to make it, after all,' she said.

'I didn't say it was difficult.'

'Ekwe, now that this is over, can you help Nkechi carry home some palm fruits tomorrow. It is not . . .'

'You can be sure I won't,' Ekwueme snapped. 'If Nkechi can't do it alone, you help her.'

'But you are free tomorrow, my son.'

'Do you mean I should never rest?'

'Ojukwu forbid! How can I ever say that?'

'Let me rest then.'

'But we need oil very badly.'

'I have promised to help tie up Ihuoma's yams tomorrow, along with Wakiri and Nnadi.'

'But I didn't know that.'

'You know now.'

'It is well, my son. Go and help Ihuoma. She is a well-behaved young woman.'

Ekwueme was secretly thrilled and excited. He went into his room light-hearted. He was not alone in admiring this woman. Everyone did so. Emenike her late husband must have been an extremely happy man. He tried to recall Emenike's disposition. Yes, he had always been happy, optimistic and pushful. But he himself had no hopes of marrying her. No? Come now, why not?

He was aroused from his reverie by the sound of a drum. He wondered whether singers were arriving from another village. He had not heard about that. He listened. A single drum beat a familiar sequence. That must be Mmam. What now? He got out of his room and saw Mmam the drummer, carrying a drum with a new skin under his left arm.

'Ekwe,' he greeted, his crooked right fingers wandering restlessly over the face of the drum.

'Mmam. You seem very happy today. Has your wife put to bed?'

'Nothing of the sort. I am from Okachuku the drum maker. He has just put on a new skin over this drum.'

'Adiele told me about it.'

'All is now set for the next dance.'

'I hope you won't burst this new skin so soon.'

'If men grow old and die, why not skins?' Mmam retorted in his quiet way.

'That is true.'

'Has the cock caught up with the moon yet?'

'I doubt it. I was up last night. The moon hid herself before the cock crew.'

'In a day or two I suppose the cock will catch her,' Mmam said, searching the sky for the moon.

'Yes.'

'Next Nkwo should be excellent then.'

'I think so too.'

'Has Adiele practised the new tune on Oji and his wife yet?'

'I suppose he has,' Ekwe said.

'Good. As for me I need no special practice.' He confirmed the statement by two bangs on the drum.

'Let's hear your new drum,' Ekwe said knowing very well that Mmam did not require a second invitation.

'Let's hear your new song,' Mmam said tightening his grip on the drum.

Ekwueme ran into the house and brought a small okwo made from a short piece of Indian bamboo. He cleared his throat and broke into the new song. He fixed his glance on Mmam's face and the latter returned the stare. It was a look of mutual understanding. A look which betrayed the secret joys they shared in making beautiful enchanting music. Children from neighbouring compounds were the first to gather. Then Nkechi and her mother came out. Lastly Wigwe drew near, smiling approval. Nkechi danced gracefully, trying to overcome one or two imperfections. Adaku danced slowly with her baby on her back. Everyone felt happy. Who could ever feel sad in the sound of such music?

CHAPTER FOURTEEN

One yam column grew after the other under the experienced hands of the trio, who were quietly directed by Nnadi. Mgbachi helped Ihuoma fetch the yams for the men. The yams were not prize-winning but they were healthy: Wakiri said they made him think of a fire, fresh pepper and fresh palm oil.

By midday, Nnadi thought it was time for a meal, but Wakiri had disappeared into the bush.

'Wakiri!' he called. 'Wakiri!' But he only succeeded in frightening little birds nesting around the neighbouring bushes.

'Wakiri!' Ekwueme took over, 'Wakiri!'

'Hei!' Wakiri shouted from the recesses of a thicket far afield, 'are you fellows crazy?'

'How long will you be?' Ekwueme queried laughing.

'No business of yours,' he shouted back.

'We are about to start eating,' Nnadi said.

'Hei, wait, I'll be back in a moment,' Wakiri shouted again. The women laughed.

'He never misses a meal,' Mgbachi said.

'Not after working so hard,' Wakiri replied, surprisingly close by.

'Chineke! Wakiri, are you here already?' Ekwueme exclaimed.

'Shut up, Ekwe.'

'We are not eating yet. We merely wanted you to come back to work,' Nnadi said.

'As if you are not hungry,' Wakiri said, 'look at your belly. It is as flat as that of a lizard. I am not even half as hungry as you are.'

The women set the meal and they sat down to eat under the shade of some palm-fronds stuck in the ground in a semicircle. At first they ate in silence, they were so hungry. Comment became more frequent as their bellies filled out and they belched more frequently. Big black ants foraged about dragging fragments of food to their nests.

'Wakiri must be dead hungry,' Ekwueme opened up, 'he can't even talk.'

For answer Wakiri explored the soup with his first and second fingers. He came across a large luscious periwinkle, attached it to his ball of foo-foo, covered the whole lot with vegetables and hauled everything into his mouth. As he swallowed there was a resounding noise in his throat.

'This is real thunder,' Nnadi said, awkwardly trying not to laugh as his mouth was full of soup.

'What is it?' Wakiri asked comically serious.

'You know,' Ekwueme said, 'it baffles me how you retain a good voice in spite of your head-of-a-baby-sized balls of foo-foo.'

'I am glad you haven't denied that I have a good voice. As for being baffled that is your affair.'

A few cups of palm wine later, the men were back to their jobs. They worked hard, bantering, whistling and singing. Now and then they mopped their brows with locally woven towels. The towels were also useful against the tse-tse flies which were numerous there in the outskirts of the forest. Nnadi had killed two, Ekwueme five and Wakiri none.

'You always let them escape,' Ekwueme said. 'Can't you even kill flies, Wakiri?'

'Just shows you are a better hunter,' Wakiri retorted.

'What has hunting got to do with the killing of tse-tse flies?'

'Are flies not animals?'

Ekwueme had no answer. He laughed.

'Judging from your keenness,' Wakiri pressed on mercilessly, 'one would think you wanted to make some soup out of them.'

'O, Wakiri, you will make us die of laughter,' Mgbachi said laughing.

As the sun travelled to Chiolu, the men and women moved homewards in single file along the narrow farm path. Ekwueme was feeling happy. He had not had any chance of really talking to Ihuoma but she had been near him all through the day. They had exchanged glances once or twice and this made him feel good and a little drowsy.

Ekwueme had tried to place himself immediately behind Ihuoma along the path going home, but somehow she had sensed his intention and had manoeuvred herself into a position two places behind him.

When they reached Ihuoma's compound they could hardly see the markings on their palms, the darkness had thickened so rapidly. They bade Ihuoma good night and left. Ekwueme took a detour and came back.

'Ekwe, I hope you will stay for the evening meal,' Ihuoma ventured, not knowing what else to say.

'Yes, if you want me to,' he mumbled absent-mindedly.

'You worked so hard today. Thank you.'

'That is nothing. I wish I could do more.'

Ihuoma had to set about her cooking and as she worked conversation became impossible. Ekwueme knew it would be thought silly and undignified to hang around the house until the food was ready.

'I am going home for a bath. I shall come back again,' he announced.

'It is well,' the woman replied.

As the young man left, his soles could be heard brushing the ground in the darkness.

The meal was over and the children had dropped to sleep one by one; Ekwueme and Ihuoma conversed aimlessly on indifferent topics. Their tones were tender and unconsciously subdued.

'Everyone knows I am interested in you,' Ekwueme said suddenly.

'Perhaps so,' she replied.

'One can't eat a crab in secret, of course.'

'Indeed not,' she said quietly.

'Now I want to come to the root of the matter.' The woman sat listening attentively.

'Ihuoma, I want to pay some bride price on you,' Ekwueme said calmly, steadily. Perhaps it was the palm wine, perhaps sheer will-power, but tonight he was a different man, poised and clear-thinking.

Ihuoma shifted her gaze to the floor. Ekwueme watched every movement she made trying to guess her reactions before she said anything. But she said nothing.

'You heard me?' Ekwueme asked.

'Yes, I did.'

'And what do you say?'

For answer Ihuoma sighed and looked squarely at him. He gazed back at her. He did not want to falter at this critical moment. At last her eyes fell.

'Ekwe,' she said at last, 'let's talk about something else.' Ek-wueme felt blank. Her language was almost insulting. Why was she so proud, so contemptuous of him? Was he so utterly unde-sirable? If she was making a fool of him, he could not help that; for him to make a fool of himself would be doubly ridiculous. Baffled and angry he rose abruptly to go.

'May the day break,' he greeted as he made for the door.

'Ekwe, sit down,' she called. But he was already outside walking away swiftly.

'Ekwe! Ekwe!!' Ihuoma called in a rather unsteady voice. Ek-wueme paused but did not turn round. Ihuoma went up to him.

'Are you angry, Ekwe?'

'No, I am not.'

'That is not true; you are angry. Come back a moment.' They went back to the house.

'Why are you angry?' she asked when they were seated. For answer Ekwueme folded his arms across his chest, leaned back on his chair and gave her a long accusing look. Then he sighed.

'Ihuoma, you are treating me like a goat.'

'Ekwe what do you want me to do? You know you are not being fair to yourself.'

'What do you mean by that?'

'Don't you understand?'

'I don't. You don't seem to be talking much sense.'

'Let's leave this matter for the moment.'

'Is that all you called me back for? All right, but explain what you mean by saying that I am not being fair to myself.'

'What about Ahurole?' Ihuoma asked looking up.

'What about her?'

'She is your fiancée and you should go ahead and marry her.'

'But I don't want to marry her.'

'Why not, she is beautiful?'

'Where is her beauty? If you are refusing me because you think I am going to marry her then you are not treating me fairly either.'

'Ekwe, I am surprised at you.'

Ekwueme stared at her. Was she really serious? Maybe it pleased her to toy with men. Maybe she was just a simpleton with as much heart as a chicken. But she was one of the most respected young women in Omokachi. Ekwueme's head started swimming.

The woman was simply incomprehensible. A curious numbness began to spread over him. He felt himself recoiling into his inner being.

'I never dreamt you were half as proud as this,' he managed to say.

'I am not proud,' she said looking away.

'Do not deny it, you are. You feel you are too good for me. You think it would be unfortunate for you to waste your beauty on a poor fellow like me. I don't blame you. I have been rash. I ought to have thought properly before making a fool of myself. Forgive me for bothering you. I will never mention this subject again.' He paused for breath.

Ihuoma's face showed signs of pain. Two small creases appeared on her face. Small as they were they carried a surprisingly deep impression of sorrow.

'Ekwe, listen,' the woman began. 'You know very well I like you. How can I deny it? You like me too, otherwise you would not want to marry me. But you need a young maiden who would obey you and give you the first fruits of her womb. Do not cheat yourself. I am too old for you. You would soon grow tired of me. My children would be a constant burden on you. No, Ekwe, I do not want to spoil your life. Since your childhood you have been engaged to Ahurole. She is young, well-behaved and beautiful. Go and marry her instead.'

Ekwueme was moved and felt his love grow even stronger for this woman.

'You know,' he said, 'my parents selected Ahurole as soon as she was born. I could hardly pull a bow by then. I really had no choice.'

'That is the usual thing. You dare not go against it. Besides, she has grown to be a pleasing girl.'

'Still she cannot be compared to you, Ihuoma. You know that very well.'

'And think of your parents, and the girl's parents too. They would be very angry with you and even more so with me. Indeed I would be the laughing-stock of all the women in the village. Ekwe, please give up the idea.'

'Ihuoma, you do not know how much respect and goodwill you command, in this village. It will go down well with them if you become my wife.'

91

'I am a woman,' she said meditatively, 'and a woman's good name can disappear overnight. What you propose can bring nothing but shame to me and regrets to you.'

'Regrets? How can a man who marries you ever regret? All your objections are based on things that just won't happen. I shall go and tell my father right away so that we can start formal negotiations.'

'Not so, Ekwe, I shall not leave my husband's compound. I intend to stay here and bring up his children. It should never be said that his compound was overrun with weeds.'

'Well,' Ekwueme said, after a long pause, 'I think we should defer this matter to some other time. Think over my proposal.'

'May the day break, Ekwe!'

'May it break.' And they parted for the night. Ekwueme walked home dejectedly. When he got home he found the compound dark. Everyone had gone to bed. But as Ekwueme fumbled with his door lock, his mother's voice startled him.

'Is that Ekwe?' she asked.

'Yes, mother.'

'You are so late, my son.'

'Mother, I rather think you went to bed too early.'

'Have you eaten?'

'I told you I would eat at Ihuoma's. You know we tied up her yams today.'

'May the day break, my son.'

'May it break, mother.'

Adaku turned uneasily in bed beside her husband and sighed.

'What is it, Adaku?' her husband asked in a voice which showed he was very wide awake.

'When shall we begin formal negotiations on Ahurole?' she asked.

'We can begin to carry palm wine to the parents around the Ige festival.'

'The sooner the better.'

'Have you any fears about Ahurole? Personally I have none. She is a good girl.'

'It is not Ahurole I am afraid of. It is Ekwe. I don't want him to get seriously involved with any woman before he gets married.'

'If you are thinking of Ihuoma, forget her. She is easily the best woman in the village. She can't do anything shameful.'

92

'So you have also noticed Ekwe's growing fondness of her.'

'I have, but it does not mean anything.'

'You can't be too sure, though.'

'Ekwe can't come to any harm. There is no need to worry.'

'You know Ihuoma is good-looking, my lord.'

'That is true.'

'And fairly young, in fact younger than Ekwe.'

'Mmm.'

'So it is possible Ekwe may begin to think of marrying her.'

'I don't think so.'

'I think so, my lord. I have a hunch and a strong one.'

'What do you want us to do?'

'We should either begin to carry wine to Ahurole's parents right away or try to discourage Ekwe from being interested in Ihuoma.'

'We can't stop him from seeing Ihuoma. He is too old for such restrictions.'

'Then we should bring Ahurole quickly, quickly.'

'Why the haste? Marriage negotiations cannot be hurried, as you know. Even if we start right now, Ahurole cannot be a member of our family until a year's time,' Wigwe said, grinding his teeth thoughtfully.

'That is just the point; we have to start early.'

'All right. I shall get some elders to go with me on the next Eke for opening talks.'

'Please do so. If Ihuoma wants to get married let her look for older married men.'

'But who told you she wants to get married?' her husband asked with undisguised irritation.

'She is a woman, my lord.'

'Then why blame her?'

'She should not pitch on our son. She is too old for him.'

'I thought you liked Ihuoma.'

'But that is not to say that Ekwe should marry her, my lord.'

'But, Adaku, who got this marriage business into your head?'

'Nobody, my lord. I just feel it.'

'Then keep quiet and don't talk about what you don't know.'

CHAPTER FIFTEEN

Slowly, and balancing her pot on her head with the confidence established by habit, Ahurole moved towards the well on a misty Nkwo morning. Her friend Titi joined her as she passed her compound. The two friends were inseparable; they fetched water and wood together, they even weeded their parents' farms together, going from one farm to the other alternately.

'Ahule,' Titi greeted her friend by a pet name.

'Titi.'

'Your indigo turned out well. It is sitting so nicely on you.'

Ahurole twisted her body this way and that to admire the indigo her mother had carefully painted on her the previous night.

'It is really nice. I am surprised at it. I am such a restless sleeper that I feared I would spoil the fine figures before they dried properly.

'So you are not as bad a sleeper as you thought after all.'

'I am. My little sister complains of blows and buffets whenever I sleep with her; so I sleep alone.'

'You should continue to sleep with your sister to get used to sharing a bed with someone.' As Titi said this she smiled mischievously and looked away.

'I don't need to share a bed with anyone,' Ahurole said with feigned indignation.

'You do.'

'I don't.'

'You do.'

'I don't.'

'You do. . . . Let's see who gives up first.'

'I have no time for endless chattering,' Ahurole said.

'Still I was right,' her friend insisted.

'How are you right?'

'Think again.'

'I won't.'

'What about Ekwe?'

'What about him?'

'I hear he will soon bring wine to your father.'

'That may be so.'

'So I am right; you should learn to share a bed with someone.'

'You are not right.'

'Will you not sleep with him when you are married?'

'I won't,' Ahurole snapped.

'You must be crazy.'

'Just wait and see.'

They got to the well and lowered specially prepared calabashes into the well by means of stout ropes. Three or four calabashes filled a normal pot. Titi helped Ahurole place her pot on her head. Titi herself had a smaller pot and needed no help.

The two friends turned back to go home. They talked less this time, being more occupied with wiping their faces as the water from their overflowing pots ran down their necks and cheeks.

'I know why you have some indigo on,' Titi began as they got near her compound. For a reply, Ahurole returned a blank expression.

'Ekwueme is coming soon, isn't he?' Titi pressed on.

'I don't know,' Ahurole replied.

'Let me know when he comes so that I can help you with the cooking.'

'I shall let you know.'

Titi walked into her compound and the friends parted. Ahurole walked on more briskly, her full breasts vibrating in unison. She was dark complexioned and the indigo she had on made her darker still. Tall and slim, she was always hoping to put on a little more flesh if only to stop her friends making annoying remarks about her flat buttocks. Her waist was heavily beaded. The beads made her hips and her behind a little fuller. Her face was beautiful, the beauty coming more from the structure of the bones than from any padding of fat. When she smiled she revealed unmarked white teeth. She had no natural gap in her teeth and fear prevented her from having one created artificially by carvers.

When she got home her mother was busy sweeping out their rooms. Her father Wagbara and little brothers were also busy sweeping away dead leaves from the compound. Even as they swept with their long brooms, leaves rained from the pear and orange trees.

'The ground will soon be littered again with these dead leaves,' Wagbara muttered,

'Nnanna, we should prune them,' Ahurole said.

'Eh, Ahule, are you back from the well?'

'Yes, Nnanna.'

'By the way, remember to keep indoors, on Eke.

'All right.'

'You don't ask me why?'

Ahurole turned round and hid her face.

'Hm, I see your mother has told you already. Still, Ekwueme and his people will be coming on Eke to knock at my door on your behalf. Your mother will tell you how to comport yourself. Go to her and find out.'

'I will do so, Nnanna,' she said and went off to the well again.

When she came back she helped her mother Wonuma prepare breakfast.

'Ahule,' her mother said 'we shall be very busy tomorrow.'

'How, mother?'

'We shall scrub the walls and floors of our house in preparation for what I told you of.'

'What else shall we do?'

'Don't worry, your father will see to the rest. He will provide the palm wine, fish and meat for the guests.'

'What about me, mother? Will I be there when the talks are being held?'

'Not all the time, my daughter. But you must look nice on that day. Already you have some indigo on. You must see to your beads in case any strings are cut. I shall give you a new wrapper. Your hair must be seen to, as well.'

'At what stage in the talks will I be required? I hope I won't have to say anything.'

'Now that I think of it, you will not be required at all at this initial stage. But of course our prospective in-laws will cast long searching glances at you at every opportunity.'

'I shall keep out of their way,' Ahurole said, pouting.

'Taaa! Don't say that. You will have to serve the entertainments, my daughter. I shall feel proud each time they look at you because I know you are one in four hundred, my dear!'

'Will Ekwueme be there?'

'I am not sure.'

'I hope he won't come along.'

'He will come eventually anyway.'

Ahurole lapsed into silence. She sat resting her chin in her right hand.

'Don't sit that way,' her mother said, 'it is unlucky. You should be happy. Cha! When I was about to be married, I remember how happy I was. My mates envied me and I was proud of your father. He was young and handsome then, and a good wrestler too. Some said he even wrestled with a huge gorilla and won.'

'I am not sad, mother. In fact I am happy. But I was wondering . . .'

'Wondering about what?'

'I really don't know.'

'Oh, don't worry. Go and get your beads and other things in order. Ekwueme is a nice boy and should make a good husband. He has never been known to be wayward and he can't suddenly change his ways now. As the saying goes, one can't learn to be left-handed in old age.'

Breakfast consisted of yam-in-palm-oil and pepper-soup with dried fish in it. Wagbara's second wife was to feed him for that day and so Wonuma and her children sat down to eat up all that they had cooked. Towards the end of the meal, Odum, Ahurole's junior brother, asked for more pepper-soup.

'The pot is almost empty,' Ahurole said. 'You should leave the rest for Ikezam.' Ikezam was the youngest boy in the family.

'Ikezam can't drink up all that soup,' Odum said, peering into the pot. 'Already his belly is so distended that it would be a wonder if it didn't burst.'

'And what of yours?' Ahurole said indignantly.

'Nne,' Odum said appealing to his mother, 'please tell her to let go the soup.'

For a moment Wonuma could not decide whom to side with.

'Ahurole, couldn't you spare him a little more soup?' she asked.

'He knows I should give him some if any were left,' Ahurole said.

'But you said you were leaving some for Ikezam,' Odum snapped.

'You should be ashamed to struggle with Ikezam over the dregs of ordinary pepper-soup,' Ahurole said with heat.

'Mark her language, mother! If she goes on I shall be compelled to deal with her.'

'She has not abused you yet, my son.'

'Are you waiting for her to abuse me outright before telling her to check her tongue?'

'Mother, why bother?' Ahurole said, 'we all know he always fights for food.'

'Look here, Ahule, don't take undue advantage of your seniority. I have had enough.'

'Will you slap me?'

'I won't but I sincerely hope your husband will give you a severe beating first thing when you get to his house.'

'Mother, do you hear him wishing me ill luck?'

'Odum, don't say that,' Wonuma intervened.

'Aha! Mother you are up and doing now. Yes, it is always so.'

'Mother, let him cry if he wants to,' Ahurole said. 'Here, Ikezam, have some more soup.'

'At this rate,' Odum said 'You will make a very stupid wife. I am happy we shall soon get rid of you. Father is as anxious as I am to see you married off.'

'Listen to that, mother,' Ahurole fumed. 'He says father wants to get rid of me. But if I am going to get married—' She got up, moved swiftly into her mother's bedroom and burst into tears.

'Ha-ha, who is crying now?' Odum said triumphantly.

'Shut up, you foul-mouthed ...' but Odum was off before his mother could get it all out.

Wonuma soothed her daughter, but not without some trouble. Ahurole had unconsciously been looking for a chance to cry. For the past year or so her frequent unprovoked sobbing had disturbed her mother. When asked why she cried, she either sobbed the more or tried to quarrel with everybody at once. She was otherwise very intelligent and dutiful. Between her weeping sessions she was cheerful, even boisterous, and her practical jokes were a bane on the lives of her friends, particularly Titi. But though intelligent, Ahurole could sometimes take alarmingly irrational lines of argument and refuse to listen to any contrary views, at least for a time. From all this her parents easily guessed that she was being unduly influenced by agwu, her personal spirit. Anyika did his best but of course the influence of agwu could not be nullified overnight. In fact it would never be completely eliminated. Everyone was mildly influenced now and then by his personal spirit. A few like Ahurole were particularly unlucky in having very troublesome spirits.

Ahurole was engaged to Ekwueme when she was eight days old,

Ekwueme was then about five years old. The initial ceremony was simple. Ekwueme's father, Wigwe, merely put some kola nuts and the shoots of young palm wine saplings into the vessel from which Ahurole drank. Thereafter he kept an eye on her casually. As both children grew they were made to understand their position. Nothing was done beyond this until the children were of age. Indeed all it meant practically was that no other suitors would bother Ahurole's father. All marriages were not contracted in this way, but when they were they flattered the parents of the girl. Clearly only the baby-girls of trusted parents could be engaged in this way.

And so Ahurole's parents were justly proud of their daughter's engagement. For years they had exercised extra care and vigilance over her. The time was come at last for formal negotiations. Negotiations might well have started two years back but Wagbara said he was not in a hurry, which implied two things: firstly that he was not too keen on his daughter's bride price, which implied he was well off; secondly that he was sure of his good influence over his daughter.

The result of this delay was that while Ahurole's mates were married and carried their first babies about and were clad in full-length wrappers, she was still wearing her maiden beads, and a small wrapper barely covering her knees. But now public opinion was beginning to weigh heavily against her continued maidenhood. One old woman living near by cleverly explained that her sobbing was not unconnected with her delayed marriage. Ahurole stoutly denied this and to add more force to her denial she wept.

On the following Nkwo evening, Wagbara sat chatting with his senior wife in her sitting-room.

'You have got everything ready for tomorrow?' Wagbara asked.

'Yes, my lord.'

'Have you given Ahule the new wrapper I bought her?'

'Yes, my lord.'

'How does she feel about it?'

'Ah, she was very delighted with it.'

'I mean the marriage.'

'It is not easy to tell. But her friend Titi told me in confidence that she is looking forward to it.'

'I am very happy to hear that.'

'I am very happy indeed, my lord. Ekwueme is such a nice young man. I am sure he will perform the duties of a husband very well.'

'No doubt, he will. Still I have not been seeing much of him lately, have you?'

'No, my lord.'

'At one time I even thought he was making a definite attempt to avoid me.'

'That cannot be so,' Wonuma said.

'I don't think so really. I wonder how it came into my mind.'

For a time husband and wife sat silently, thinking about their daughter.

'My lord, your meal is ready.'

Wagbara looked up. Aleruchi his second wife was at the door.

'I am coming,' he said.

'Please come soon, my lord, or the foo-foo may get hardened. You know the harmattan is on.'

'I wonder what the world is coming to. It is rather late in the year for the harmattan.'

'They say the king of the Wakanchis is dead and that they are producing the harmattan to preserve the corpse until human heads are procured for the burial.'

'Ha-ha, I have heard this silly story. I am sure that fool Wakiri the wag of Omokachi is behind it all.'

'Do you mean it is not true, my lord?'

'Of course not.'

'Many have confirmed it.'

'Yes, many like you. Women believe anything.'

'But it sounds credible, my lord.'

'Oyirim,' Wagbara said addressing his wife fondly, 'no one can control the harmattan, not even Wakanchis.'

'Of course you must be right. I don't know which is which.'

'But, my lord, I thought you said some time ago that the Wakanchis controlled the harmattan?' Wonuma put in.

'Not me. What I said was that the Wakanchis are a race of dwarfs skilled in medicine and other mysterious powers. They can control the direction of the wind but they cannot start or stop it. If for instance they find the harmattan is getting very uncomfortable they can divert it to their neighbours who will then have a double share of the cold wind.'

'My lord, this is very interesting,' Aleruchi said. 'I wonder how you get to know these wonderful things.'

'In my youth, that is before I married Wonuma, I travelled quite extensively. Why, I very nearly reached the farm land of the Wakanchis myself.'

Wonuma sensed that her husband was all set on a long discourse.

'You should go and eat, my lord,' she said. 'It is getting rather late.'

'Indeed,' he said, and walked off with his junior wife. He washed his hands and touched the foo-foo.

'Chei! This is stone!'

'My lord, it is the fault of the harmattan.' Aleruchi pleaded.

CHAPTER SIXTEEN

Ekwueme came home from his traps feeling downcast. He had caught two animals and sold them on the way home but that did not make him any more cheerful. His mind was weighing the possible marriage with Ahurole. For the past few days he had been giving evasive and vague answers whenever the subject came up. His father did not notice it. He knew that by custom it was his sole responsibility to get his son his first wife. His son would hardly come into the picture until the bride was almost home. Still it would be a good idea to take Ekwueme along for the opening talks. He could loiter around and joke with the other young men.

So when Ekwueme came home that morning his father spoke about it.

'Ekwe, tomorrow is the great day.'

'Yes, Nnanna, but I may not go with you.'

'Of course you will. Don't tell me you're shy at your age.'

'Certainly not, Nnanna.'

'I have asked Wakiri to help carry the calabash of wine. You will merely stroll along with us.'

'In that case, I don't need to come along at all.'

'But what will you do tomorrow?'

'My traps are in a bad state of repair, father.'

At this stage Wigwe began to watch his son closely. As he watched him, Ekwueme frowned unconsciously. As tension mounted Ekwueme turned round and entered his room. Puzzled, Wigwe retired immediately to his reception hut, his brow furrowed with misgivings.

'Adaku!'

'Yes, my lord.'

'Come!'

His wife came up, looked at his face and sat down beside him. She knew immediately that whatever was on his mind could not be discussed standing up.

'Have you discussed tomorrow's arrangements with your son?' Wigwe asked, grinding his teeth in a slow deliberative rhythm.

'I have not.'

'Go and find out what is wrong with him. It will take me a longer time to get at the root of the matter.'

'What matter?'

'Go and have a chat with him, I say.'

'Yes, my lord.'

The mystified woman went into her son's room. She found him sitting on his three-legged chair, his chin pillowed in his palms.

'What is wrong, my son?' she asked, peering apprehensively into his troubled face.

'Please tell father I don't want to marry Ahurole.'

'Amadioha forbid! Don't say it again. Whoever heard of this type of thing? Tell me what doubts you have. I am sure I shall clear them at once.'

'I have no doubts about Ahurole,' Ekwueme said, his chin still in his palms.

'Then what is it, oh what is it?'

'It is just what I have said. I don't want to marry her.'

'But why? You can't sit there placidly to say such disturbing things without proper explanations.'

'I want to wait a little before getting married.'

Adaku soon realized that she would gain nothing by getting angry. She moved nearer her son and placed an arm round his hunched shoulders.

'Ekwe, my darling, speak your mind. I am your mother and cannot let you down. I should be the last person to force you into any unpleasant situation. Your father is to be feared, I know, but I can hold my own when I mean to.'

'Mother, my reasons are simple, I don't want to get married just yet.'

'But Ekwe you know that negotiations will last a year. Ahurole will not be here permanently till then.'

'I know that,' her son replied implacably.

Adaku was getting to her wits' end.

'Is Ahurole not beautiful.'

'She is quite beautiful.'

'Is she too slim for your liking?'

'I hate fat girls.'

'Do you doubt her purity?'

'No.'

'Has she offended you in any way?'

'How could she when she does not live near us?'

'Are her parents hostile to you?'

'Not at all.'

Adaku turned round and faced the wall. Her tears flowed fast. Her sobs were isolated but heavy. To disappoint Ahurole and her parents would be a terrible blot on them. The shame would be crushing. Whoever broke a childhood engagement? The situation was desperate.

Her sobbing made Ekwueme very uncomfortable. He loved his mother dearly though he could be firm with her when he thought fit.

'Mother, there is no need to cry,' he managed to say.

'No need to cry when you have made our family a laughing-stock? Chei! Ekwe, my son, what has gone into your mind?'

Ekwueme declined to say anything further. He was getting a little confused himself. He was beginning to realize that he was causing a serious crisis. His father's controlled reactions and his mother's outbursts all showed that clearly enough. But he felt that if he could stand firm now he might have his way.

For some time mother and son sat motionless in the small room. The sun sent two straight red shafts through holes in the roof. Outside a black and white goat heavy with child sauntered across. It stopped by the doorway, looked intently at the pair of unhappy human beings inside and moved on to forage for food. Adaku blew her nose, wiped her red eyes and studied the floor. Her toes twitched as her thoughts darted this way and that. Here was a real mystery. Most young men would be impatient over a girl like Ahurole. What had come over Ekwe? Someone must be involved. He must have been bewitched. If so Anyika would soon set that right. But if Ekwueme had not been bewitched, what then? Maybe Ekwe was interested in another girl, but who? Ah! What a fool she was. Ihuoma, of course. It was just as she feared.

Having arrived at this conclusion she felt calmer. Ihuoma should not to be too difficult to deal with. She cleared her throat and as casually as it was possible she tried another line.

'Ekwe, by the breasts that fed you, and by the laps that carried you, I command you to answer this question truthfully. Have you any other girl in mind?'

Ekwueme knew his mother was in desperate earnest now. She had bound him by highly sacred things,

'Yes,' he answered steadily.

'Who is she?'

'Ihuoma.'

'I have always thought that woman was up to no good. How right I was.'

'Please do not blame her.'

Adaku fought to control her temper. She knew it would merely drive her son desperate.

'Ekwe, do you realize that she has three children and that she is too old for you to marry.'

'I am older than she is.'

'I know, but she is too old for you to marry.'

'She is young enough.'

'Who will maintain her children?'

'She and I.'

'Well, my son, I am much overcome. My day is turning into darkness. I shall leave you to think over the situation. One thing is certain, it would be a terrible mistake to marry Ihuoma. I know. . . .' The unhappy woman checked herself at that point. She wanted to add that Ihuoma must have fed him with a strong love potion, but she knew that would merely infuriate him. Still the fact was glaringly clear and it was just a question of getting an antidote from Anyika to clear up the stupid ideas in her son's head. She went to her husband and related the interview.

'Do you remember the argument we had about Ihuoma?' she asked half triumphantly.

'Yes.'

'Women are not always fools.'

'That is true, but I still think Ihuoma is not to blame. Ekwueme is just foolish or should I say childish.'

'My lord, our son is definitely under the the influence of a love potion. All we need do is find an antidote and quickly too.'

'Oh, you mean Ihuoma has given him a potion?'

'That is very clear, my lord. We shall see Anyika today.'

'Go and do your cooking.'

Wigwe sat in his reception hall thinking. He could share his son's feelings to a certain extent. He really could not blame him very seriously. Ihuoma was very beautiful. Everyone knew it. It was understandable that her mature beauty should turn any man's head. Still a young man needed a maiden. What was more, to break

105

faith with Wagbara was unthinkable. No, there was only one way.

The more Wigwe thought about Ihuoma, the stronger grew his conviction that she would never accept his son's offer of marriage no matter how much she might like him. She was a young woman of great moral courage and would rather die than do anything that would hurt anyone seriously. She was even less likely to do anything that would bring public ridicule on her. If he was right, then the problem was easy to solve. He would interview Ihuoma in his son's presence. Her refusal would be a blow big enough to make Ekwueme realize his folly.

Wigwe's relationship with his son Ekwueme was one of mutual respect. There were two reasons for this; firstly, he could no longer give him a thrashing or even scold him openly on serious matters; secondly, Ekwueme was dutiful and sensible. He was hard working, a very good singer and not a bad wrestler. He was a son anyone could be proud of. Of course Wigwe had full authority over his son but he hoped he would never be called upon to exert this authority in any unpleasant situation. On his part Ekwueme had a vague feeling he could thwart his father's authority if the worst came to the worst, but like his father he hoped such an occasion would never arise.

When therefore Wigwe detected signs of his son's aversion to the proposed marriage he was for a time at a loss as to what to do. But when he weighed the possible repercussions of breaking off his son's long-standing engagement he grew resolute. Delicate matters were best discussed late at night or early in the morning, but as the marriage negotiations were to begin the next day there was no time to be lost. He summoned his son to the reception hall where he had been sitting. Sensing that neighbours passing by would distract him with their greetings he decided to go into his room. Ekwueme followed him, breathing deeply.

'Now, Ekwe,' he said, 'what were you telling your mother?' His tone was such that Ekwueme began to realize that he was causing great pain to his father. He felt a little guilty.

'Dede, I really don't know how to say it but I do not want to marry Ahurole.'

'Whom do you want to marry?'

'Ihuoma.'

'Do you realize that Ahurole was engaged to you almost twenty years ago?'

106

'I do.'

'What is wrong with Ahurole?'

'Nothing.'

'Is Ihuoma more beautiful than she is?'

'I can't tell.'

'Listen my son, you must not be like the caterpillar that holds fast to tree branches when small but loses its grip and falls to its death when much older. So far you have showed all signs of growing into a sensible young man. If at this critical stage you turn into a fool, it will be most unfortunate. I do not say there is anything wrong with Ihuoma. She is a good young woman, but nevertheless a wrong choice for you. She has three children. She is looking after her late husband's compound. Her allegiance to you would take second place. Remember that a hen cannot scratch for food with her two legs simultaneously. Be sensible. Tomorrow I am going to start negotiations on Ahurole. I have informed her parents and relations. Everything is ready. We can't go back. I tell you it is almost an abomination to break off an engagement like this. It is unheard of. No one would ever side with you.'

Ekwueme's heart jumped into his stomach. A sickening sensation assailed him. His father was right, of course. Worse, tradition was decidedly against him and the thought of kicking against it unnerved him. It would be sensational news in the village. Then he thought of Ihuoma. Suddenly his father was no longer there. In his place Ihuoma stood smiling wistfully, a deep affection glowing in her eyes. Energy surged through him and his eyes shone. His father's voice recalled him to reality.

'Go now and prepare for tomorrow,' it said.

'Dede, I have never disregarded your words. Can't you bear with me this once?' Ekwueme pleaded. 'I am not altogether a fool. My eyes are open. I have thought over this matter for a long time and I am sure Ihuoma will do.'

'Do you mean you are still insisting?'

Wigwe was getting worked up now, but he managed to control himself. He himself hated taking dictation from anyone and he knew that his son resembled him both physically and emotionally.

'I really cannot help wanting to marry Ihuoma,' his son replied.

'Come, have you ever asked her to marry you?'

'I have.'

'And did she consent?'

'She did,' he lied.

'I do not believe you. Ihuoma is too sensible for that unless everyone is going crazy. Unless I hear from her I cannot be convinced. So this evening we shall both call on her and find out her feelings on the matter. You will soon realize your mistake. I shall postpone negotiations to the next Great Eke, eight days hence. Fetch me Mmam. He will carry the message to Ahurole's parents.'

Ekwueme left his father gloomier than before. There was no telling what Ihuoma's reactions would be. She had refused him once and with good reasons. She might do it again and make him look childish. The only way was to go and plead with her.

He rushed off to fetch Mmam the drummer for his father. When he came back he went straight to Ihuoma. But her compound was deserted. He went back to his house, changed into his hunting wrapper, and made for Ihuoma's farm. But her farm was deserted too. As he was about to turn back Nnenda, Ihuoma's neighbour, came up.

'Where is Ihuoma?' he asked without returning her greetings.

She stared at him curiously.

'Has anything gone wrong?' she asked.

'No, but where is she?' He barely refrained from shouting.

'She went to Omigwe to see her parents.'

'When will she be back?'

'She did not say, but possibly tomorrow.'

Ekwueme headed for home leaving Nnenda bewildered.

Once home he changed and set off for Omigwe. He threw all cares to the wind. He would go straight to her parents' house and speak to her. He might even tell her parents right away.

On his way he met Mmam as he was coming back from his errand.

'Did you see Ahurole's parents?' Ekwueme asked.

'Yes, and I have relayed the message. Wagbara felt very disappointed and demanded explanations. I was forced to lie. I said your father was not feeling very well. I must hurry home and brief him on the lie.'

Moving swiftly, Ekwueme soon came to Omigwe. He had to pass Wagbara's compound before reaching Ihuoma's parents' compound. Fortunately no one saw him. When he came to Ogbuji's compound he saw Nwonna and other children playing.

'Where is your mother?' he demanded.

But Nwonna paid no attention as he dodged this way and that with his mates in hot pursuit. They were engaged in a game the essence of which was to determine who would touch the other last. He had touched a playmate and was racing away, when he bumped into Ekwueme.

'Hei, Ekwe, are you here?' he piped.

'Where is your mother?' Ekwueme asked.

'She's gone to farm with grandmother. They say the farm is very far, otherwise I should have gone with them.'

'When will they come back?'

'After work.'

'What time, you fool?'

This aggression puzzled Nwonna who was used to Ekwueme's gentleness.

'Ekwe, please, I don't know,' he answered and dashed off after his friends. To go after Ihuoma any further was unwise. It would be ludicrous appearing suddenly in Ogbuji's farm and asking for his daughter. No, he would have to depend on luck.

CHAPTER SEVENTEEN

Ihuoma came back to Omokachi that evening. As soon as her neighbour Nnenda sensed her presence she came over to greet her.

'You look tired, you must have worked hard,' Nnenda said.

'It was not so much the work as the distance I trekked that has made me tired,' Ihuoma replied languidly. 'The farm was so far that although we ate before setting out, we had to eat again as soon as we arrived before we could do any work.'

'Do they lack land? Why should the farm be so far?'

'No, my father has a lot of land, but the land over the stream is much more fertile. You know the stream I mean?'

'No.'

'It is Mini Wekwu.'

'The one that separates us from Chiolu?'

'Yes.'

'Does it extend that way?'

'Yes, it is even broader there.'

'How did you cross it?'

'With rafts.'

'Hei, that is a funny way of travelling to one's farm. Were you not afraid?'

'No, the stream is not deep.'

'You should have forded it then.'

'That would mean being wet to the breasts or even to the neck.'

'Will you go back tomorrow?'

'Tomorrow is Eke,' Ihuoma said.

'That is true. I had forgotten. I was even thinking of going to work tomorrow.'

'You will have to go on the day after tomorrow then, that is on Irie.'

'Yes, that reminds me of Ekwueme. He was at your farm today looking for you.'

'What for?'

'He did not say.'

'Maybe he was just passing by.'

'Perhaps.'

Nnenda was sure that Ekwueme had gone to the farm specifically to look for Ihuoma. She also felt that he was desperate over something; but she did not tell her friend all this. Intimate as they were, she still knew how far she could go into her affairs.

'Let me hurry home. My husband may begin to miss me.'

'You are right. Men are jealous at all ages,' Ihuoma replied smiling.

Ihuoma pondered over Ekwueme's search for her at the farm. As she put the children to bed she tried to puzzle out the reasons behind his movements. Nothing occurred to her. She had told him in fairly plain terms that marriage between them was impossible. He had promised, even though in anger, not to mention the subject again. What then was this new development?

Ihuoma had supped with her parents before coming back. She only had to go to bed. She was about to put out her oil lamp when she heard a knock at her door. It must be Nnadi, her brother-in-law, she thought.

'Is that Nnadi?' she asked.

'No, my daughter, it is Wigwe.'

She recognized the voice and was rather disconcerted. Her mind flashed back to Ekwueme's movements as related by Nnenda and her heart sank. Clearly all was not well.

'Dede, is anything wrong?'

'No, my daughter, I merely want to see you.'

She opened the door as calmly as she could. When she saw Ekwueme by his father's side her perplexity became noticeable.

'Ekwe.'

'Ihuoma.'

She offered them seats and then sat on the sleeping mound opposite the men. The oil lamp on a ledge in the wall threw grotesque shadows of the men on the wall behind them. Now Wigwe's head was long and thin, now fat and short as the flame flickered. All was quiet save for the regular breathing of the children in the next room.

'Dede, this night visit is so unusual; I was almost afraid something had gone wrong,' Ihuoma managed to say.

'All is well, my daughter. I came to find the answer to a little problem.'

The old man ground his teeth gently as he spoke. He was evidently weighing his words carefully.

'In a way,' Wigwe began again, 'this visit is unusual, but I believe it is the only way to solve the little problem in my mind. True, you are merely a woman but your good behaviour has placed you a little above many other women in the village. When a child washes his hands he may dine with his elders. To come to the point, my visit is in connection with your relationship with my son Ekwueme. I didn't know anything about this relationship until it cropped up today during some important family discussions.'

Ihuoma was now fully aware of what to expect. Ekwueme shuffled his legs to attract her attention. She looked up and saw the awful plea in his eyes. She was overcome but managed to keep a steady head. Presently there was a knock at the door. It turned out to be Nnadi. Ihuoma was not sure whether or not her brother-in-law's presence relieved her. Nnadi was surprised to find Wigwe and his son there so late. But he overcame his surprise superbly.

'Wigwe.'

'Nnadi.'

'Ekwe.'

'Mm, Nnadi.'

'I didn't know you were the people I saw walking into the compound. I thought it proper to check since Ihuoma is the only woman in the compound.'

'We are indeed,' Wigwe said. 'You did well to come. You ought to safeguard your sister-in-law against bad men.'

'I am relieved now. I think I should go back.'

'It is well,' Wigwe said.

Nnadi picked up his matchet which he had left leaning against the wall, and disappeared into the darkness shutting the door behind him. He knew it would be mean to inject himself into a conference to which he was not invited. He had acted up to the accepted code of conduct. But his coming made Wigwe think again. He had come to find out from Ihuoma whether his son had proposed to her and if so what her answer was. Nnadi's arrival reminded him forcibly that such a procedure was improper without Ihuoma's people being around. He realized he had no right to question her that way. It would appear he was taking undue advantage of her widowhood. It was persecution. Nnadi would certainly be angry if he knew about it later on.

112

What then? He could not go back without saying something. For a time his mind was in a whirl. The silence grew distressing.

'Ihuoma, my child,' Wigwe began at last, 'really I ought to have come here with more people, but I have avoided formalities because I want to spare myself any embarrassments. Formalities will come later if all goes well. Please don't blame me.'

Ihuoma, not knowing exactly what was coming this time, had no comments to make. She sat upright and directed her gaze meekly to the floor. That was the correct posture to adopt when being spoken to by an elder. She was desperately trying to be as blameless as possible in what was threatening to be a complicated state of affairs.

'Ihuoma,' Wigwe resumed, 'I have come to ask you to marry my son Ekwueme. What do you say?'

Ekwueme looked up, his face lined with surprise. A moment later he realized his father was being supremely tactful. The irony of it all embittered him. Ihuoma saw the ruse immediately and was saddened at this play-acting at her own expense. Even a fool would not let his son take on a widow as a first wife. Did Wigwe think she was too naïve to see through that?

'Dede,' Ihuoma replied steadily, 'I thank you for this proposal. It is a good one, but I cannot accept it because I want to stay in my late husband's compound and bring up his children to carry on his name. I hope Ekwe will not take it ill and that he will find a good girl to marry soon.'

Of course Wigwe did not expect anything else. He did not try to persuade her. That would be over-acting. Bidding her good morrow he and his son rose to go.

Completely humiliated, Ekwueme strode ahead of his father, boiling with indignation, not against Ihuoma, but against his father for this wicked contrivance. He had been portrayed as a silly child who did not know what was good for him. To keep back the tears stretched his manliness to the utmost.

He went to bed quietly and had a restless night. In between nightmares he tried to think of a new line of action. His efforts were abortive. He rose early the next morning and went off to his traps before anyone was awake. He did not want to see his father, at least for a time.

When the sun began to sink to Chiolu he was still not back. His father grew alarmed. He knew he had made things very difficult for his son and began to relent. On the other hand he was happy he had solved the problem once and for all.

'My lord, Ekwe is not back yet,' Adaku said supporting the back of her head with her two palms, having dovetailed the fingers into one another.

'Is his house still locked?' Wigwe asked.

'It is, my lord.'

'Well, he will come back in his own good time. He knows the forest too well to be lost in it.' But behind Wigwe's mind a nagging anxiety was growing.

Adaku for her part could no longer concentrate on her cooking. Her daughter Nkechi took charge.

'Did you say anything annoying to Ekwe last night?'

'I didn't. Haven't I related the whole thing to you?'

'You have, my lord. I was just wondering why Ekwe should stay so long in the bush. The sun is going to Chiolu and he has had no meal since morning.'

'Calm yourself, Adaku. Even if he is annoyed that is no reason he should run away from home. He would only prove himself a woman. He won't run away, unless I am not his father.'

'Of course you are his father, my lord,' the woman said.

'Then he will come back. It is not in our blood to run away from difficulties.'

'There he comes!' Adaku exclaimed. Wigwe looked up and saw his son turning into the compound with a huge deer slung across his back.

'Welcome, Ekwe!'

'Mm, Dede,' the young man replied.

'You have been away so long, my son,' his mother said, 'you almost frightened me. What a mighty animal you've got.'

'It is really big; well done, Ekwe.' Wigwe examined the antlers of the creature. 'We shall keep the skull in our reception hall. This is the biggest animal you've ever killed.'

Wigwe helped his son skin the deer carefully. The brown fur was dotted with white spots and was worth preserving. They cut up the body of the deer. Adaku made a big fire under the bamboo raft on which the meat was placed to smoke. The skull was carefully carved and when every trace of meat on it had disappeared it shone.

'We shall place it on the roof to dry,' Ekwueme said.

114

'No my son, the vultures will deface it or even carry it off. Place it over the fire.'

As father and son worked hand in hand, the bitterness of the previous night grew lighter. Ekwe's drawn face relaxed somewhat.

*

When Wigwe and his son left Ihuoma, she locked her door and wept. Her sobbing was silent but extremely bitter. For the first time since her husband died her courage seemed to desert her. Her plight was made worse by the fact that she was very reluctant to confide in anyone. She bore her sorrows alone. She was her own comforter and adviser.

Presently she fell asleep. Some unwiped tears dried and left greasy tracks on her face. Her heaving breast resumed its normal breathing and she slept on peacefully. She woke in the morning with a headache and a slight dizziness. She decided to stay indoors the whole day. As it was an Eke her decision was in fact unnecessary; she could not in any case go to the farm to work.

After the morning meal she lay on the sleeping mound in her sitting-room. Nwonna took the second child out to play and she was left with the youngest. Her headache grew worse. She rose, went into the kitchen behind the house and extracted from over the fireplace a grey piece of what looked like ordinary clay but was in fact a medicine for headache. She chipped off a small bit and with some water made it into a paste. She then rubbed this on her forehead and occiput. The medicine had some pepper in it and soon she began to sweat. Still her head seemed to be coming apart. She tied a piece of cloth tightly round it and lay down again. The throb in her head dulled her senses. It seemed her head contained a mad drummer relentlessly beating a monotonous tattoo. The events of the past night raced through her mind in a confused blur. She fell into a troubled sleep which never deepened into real slumber. She was dreaming but felt she was controlling her dreams which were all focused on Wigwe.

Who ever heard of such a stupid marriage proposal? She mused. It was the greatest insult she had ever had to bear. It was amazing that an old man of Wigwe's standing should do a thing like that: rushing up to her late in the night without notice and with none of her people around. The more she thought about it the angrier she

115

grew. Her cogitations mingled with her dreams and at one stage she was fighting with Wigwe amidst the shouts of bystanders.

Suddenly she woke and found Nwonna standing by her bed and shouting at her to wake up. He was waving a parcel in the air excitedly with his right hand and was shaking her up with his left.

'What is it?' the woman asked, wiping sweat off her face.

'It is meat, very big meat from Ekwe.'

'Let me see.' Ihuoma undid the parcel and a huge piece of meat met her gaze. For a long time she looked at it. At last Nwonna got tired of jumping up and down excitedly and watched his mother. His enthusiasm was somewhat damped by her worried looks. He was old enough to appreciate her various moods.

'How did he give it to you?'

'I ran an errand for him. He gave me some parcels to deliver to Wodu Wakiri and Mmam-with-the-crooked-fingers. When I came back he gave me the meat.'

'It is wrong to receive gifts when you run errands for people.'

'I did not ask for it,' the distressed child replied.

'That is true, but you probably waited too long.'

'I did not wait.'

'You did, don't do it again.' Ihuoma was being very unfair and she knew it. The gift was obviously meant for her and she was mortified. She let loose her annoyance on her son.

Her first impulse was to throw away the gift far, far, into the bush, but on second thoughts she went over to the kitchen and stored it in her basket of venisons. When she came back Nwonna was nowhere to be seen. She went outside and found him leaning against the wall. He was wiping one red eye after the other trying to keep his tears back. His mother went up to him and put her arms around him; it triggered off his pent-up feelings and he wept aloud, the sobs shaking him violently. Ihuoma tried to wipe his eyes with a corner of her wrapper, but he shook her off and moved a little way. She closed in on him again and held him fast this time. She caressed him and called him many fond names.

'Hush Nyeoma, Okpara, Agu, Little Master, Rat-killer!' This last name amused Nwonna and very reluctantly he smiled and eventually laughed through his tears.

CHAPTER EIGHTEEN

It was clever of Wigwe to have thought of that interview. But it was also a thing he ought not to have done. In a way it was beneath him and he knew he had earned Ihuoma's contempt. But a father's primary duty to his son was to get him as good a wife as the neighbourhood could boast of. If in the attempt he made a few people unhappy, that was hard luck.

Ekwueme now had no reasons for insisting on marrying Ihuoma. She had rejected him – in front of his father – although he was convinced that she would willingly marry him under normal circumstances. The piece of meat he sent her was meant to convey to her the fact that he fully grasped the situation and had no ill feelings whatsoever against her and that if anything she had by her discretion and show of decorum installed herself more firmly in his mind.

But it was clear that Ihuoma was now beyond him. The more Ekwueme thought about this the more depressed he grew. He dreaded going for the negotiations over Ahurole. He had to. No one had ever turned down a childhood engagement. The whole village would side with his father and pour scorn on him. The high esteem in which the elders held him would be swept away. The situation reminded him of a story about the tortoise whose trap had caught an impossible fairy in the form of an animal. If he took the animal away he was to die. If he set it free he was still to die.

The next Eke found Wigwe, Mmam, Wakiri and Ekwueme marching in single file towards Omigwe. Wakiri carried the single calabash of wine needed for the opening talks. Ekwueme brought up the rear. He was chewing a blade of grass and occasionally amused himself by watching Wakiri's knock-kneed legs.

'Go on, what are you turning round for?' Ekwueme demanded.

'To make sure you're coming.'

'I am not a baby.'

'Then why are you chewing that blade of grass?'

'It is not reserved for babies only.'

'You're right. It is for babies and goats.'

'Wakiri, I simply haven't got the breath for you this morning. Let me be, please.' Wakiri stopped and barred Ekwueme's way.

'You don't look happy, Ekwe. What is it?' Wakiri searched his friend's face.

'One can't be happy all the time,' Ekwe replied evasively.

'But surely you ought to be happy today.'

'I know I should.'

'You should indeed. If you showed up with that face at Omigwe, it would be terrible. Why, it is just as if you have been taking some raw yams.' Ekwueme laughed and the blade of grass fell off his mouth.

Wigwe and Mmam realized that the other two were not following up. They turned round.

'What is holding you up?' Wigwe shouted at them.

'I was adjusting the keg of wine on my head,' Wakiri lied.

'If you are tired, hand it over to Mmam,' the old man replied.

'Yes, indeed, let me help you,' Mmam said.

'Help indeed, when Omigwe is in sight. Why did you not speak up all this time, you old trickster?'

They arrived at Omigwe. Wagbara was at his reception hall chatting with his brother Nwenike. He rose to meet the visitors. When he saw Wakiri, an imperceptible frown crept into his face. He hated having to deal with clowns. He thought Wigwe knew better than to bring the loud-mouthed Wakiri along. He conducted his visitors into his sitting-room and hailed his wife.

'Wonuma! Wonuma!' His voice echoed back so distinctly that Wigwe and his train could not help noticing it.

'What a nice thing you have got here,' Wakiri said. 'The echo has helped you call your wife four times.' All except Wagbara laughed.

'It is the clump of trees behind the compound that does it,' Wagbara said evenly. He would just have to put this fellow in his place. His daughter's marriage was certainly not the occasion for childish jokes. Wonuma came in. She greeted Wigwe and his train amiably. She gave Wakiri special notice.

'Ah, Wodu, you are here!'

'Do you think so?' Wakiri retorted scratching his chin. Again well-formed teeth flashed in all directions. Wagbara called Wigwe aside.

'Why did you bring this fellow in a serious thing of this nature?' he asked indignantly.

'Do you mean Wakiri?'

'Of course, who else?'

'You don't like him?'

'He is too childish.'

'He's a joker all right, but he can be amazingly level-headed.'

'I don't know about that. Please don't come with him again.'

'If you object, I shall leave him behind next time.'

The two old men joined the others and conversation flowed on again. Presently Wonuma brought in a calabash of carefully pounded yam. Her daughter Ahurole brought in another. She gave a general greeting and walked out quickly. In that brief appearance Ekwueme took in many details. Ahurole was pretty. There was no doubt there. As for her slimness, that would be an old story after her first child. Her waist was heavily bedecked with large beads and a beautiful new wrapper just failed to cover her knees. She also had beads at the knees and around her neck. Her lithe bare body showed disappearing marks of indigo which her mother had put on her some eight days before. Her breasts stood firm and defiant. The ojongo hair style became her well. When she went out, the men avoided looking at each other. No one wanted to betray his admiration. There was silence for a time.

They ate in two groups. Wagbara, Wigwe and Nwenike shared one calabash while the young men attacked the other. Ekwueme did not feel hungry. He made his balls of foo-foo very small and ate slowly. But why should he really bother? His father was right after all. Ahurole was good enough for any man. Each time she came in he watched her intently. He couldn't quite say who was more beautiful now, Ihuoma or Ahurole. Admittedly Ihuoma's beauty was more rounded and mature. She walked with grace and rare assurance. But Ahurole's features had the firmness of her youth and her steps were elastic. There was shyness curiously mingled with defiance in her face and Ekwueme realized instinctively that he would have much to contend with.

After the meal, Wagbara served his guests with palm wine. Wakiri smacked his lips and belched contentedly.

'You must have excellent tappers here,' he said. 'The blend of nche is unbeatable.'

'It is quite good,' Wagbara grunted.

119

'This must be a "home" tree,' Wakiri said.

'No, it is tapped from a tree in the Great Ponds,' Wagbara replied in a matter-of-fact way.

'Chineke! You must have worn off many a tapping chisel by now.' Wagbara smiled faintly.

'Do you do any tapping yourself?' he asked condescendingly.

'I used to,' Wakiri said, 'but I stopped because I feared I would become a drunkard.'

'That is wrong,' Mmam put in. 'He stopped when some bees stung him and he fell off a tree.'

They had a good laugh at Wakiri but he himself laughed most and added:

'When I came back my mother could not recognize me by looking at my face; she had to look at my legs.' And now Wagbara laughed in spite of himself. Well, there was no harm after all in having the fellow around.

The meal over, the serious part of their mission began. At a glance from Wigwe, Mmam brought the keg of palm wine closer. Wigwe placed it carefully in the centre of the little group.

'Wagbara, my friend,' Wigwe began, 'I have come to ask for permission to begin negotiations for a marriage between our two children. But first things first, here is the keg of palm wine.'

There was a hush in the room. Everyone concentrated his gaze on the keg of palm wine like Nwokekoro gazing on the shrine of Amadioha. It was a solemn occasion. At last Wagbara stirred and shifted his gaze from the wine to the face of his prospective in-law.

'Wigwe, you have always been my friend. You are a man to be respected. You have my permission.' They drank the wine slowly with very little conversation.

'Who will be my guide during the negotiations?' Wigwe asked.

'Nwenike will be your right-hand man. I have given him this honour not only because he is my younger brother but also because on the day Ahurole was born he played a role I shall never forget. I was away hunting when labour pains began to torment Wonuma. Nwenike called in Ndalu, that infallible expert on childbirth, paid the fees and saw to every other thing. After the birth of the child he rushed to the bush and with uncanny intuition found me in a remote corner of the thick forest by the Great Ponds.'

During this recital Nwenike's face was set in a painful type of

120

smile. His difficulty arose from the fact that he did not know exactly what facial expression was best suited for such an occasion. At the end of the tribute paid him he cleared his throat.

'It is a pleasure for me to be your guide in the negotiation,' he said. 'I have always regarded Ahurole as my daughter.'

In a marriage a guide is a very important fellow. He introduces the prospective bridegroom (or his representative) to important relations of the bride. He gives him a good idea as to their order of importance. More important still he fights tooth and nail to slash down the bride price. Although related to the bride, he is expected to side with the bridegroom in all things. The choice of a guide makes all the difference in marriage proceedings.

This was as far as they could go on that day. Wigwe and his train retired to Nwenike's house to greet his household. From now on Wigwe would not hold any talks with Wagbara directly. Nwenike would always be present and would play host to Wigwe each time he came for further talks.

*

Gradually Ekwueme's respect for married men grew as they made more and more journeys to Omigwe. They accomplished very little on each occasion but it cost them no small amount of money. For one thing they carried three kegs of palm wine on each subsequent visit; for another Ahurole's relations were by no means few and many of them were entitled to something from them. During the journeys Ekwueme saw little of Ahurole. Wonuma his mother-in-law did her best to bring them together, but Ahurole was most evasive. On their fourth journey, Ekwueme decided to have a talk, no matter how short, with his bride-to-be. After the usual entertainments, he left his father and went in search of Ahurole. She was in her mother's sitting-room with her friend Titi who was plaiting her hair. Ekwueme sat down on a small mound and faced the two girls. Ahurole promptly got up and disappeared. Shyness in a bride was usual and understandable but Ekwueme wondered if this was not going too far.

'Don't worry,' Titi said soothingly, 'I shall fetch her in a moment.' She went behind the yard and found her friend in the kitchen.

'Why did you run away?' Titi asked. 'You are behaving like a child.'

'What do you want me to do?'

'Stay in the room, of course, and chat with him.'

'Well, I won't.'

'Just tell me why.'

'Would you stay if you were in my place?'

'With pleasure.'

'I bet you won't.'

'I will.'

'You won't.'

'I will. Come, let's go back. He won't eat you. You know Ekwe is gentle and soft-spoken, unlike some loud-mouthed young men I know. Come, Ahule, you won't be alone with him, I will be there.'

'I have told you I won't go,' Ahurole sulked. Exasperated, Titi went to look for her mother. She thought she might bully her into submission.

'Just like her,' Wonuma said after Titi had related the incident, 'I never can understand this stubborn child. She never seems to grow up in things like this. Her agwu is her main stumbling block.' But like all mothers she knew threats would not do.

'Ahule, my dear child,' she said, 'don't behave this way. You only make wrong impressions on your husband.'

'I don't care, let him go home if he wants to.'

'Hush, lower your tone, he may overhear you. Come with me and you will see how simple it is.'

Titi and Wonuma half-dragged Ahurole into the room. Ekwueme was laughing softly.

'When will this hide-and-seek stop?' he said teasingly. For answer Ahurole turned her face to the wall and her friend continued the hair plaiting. Ekwueme, finding conversation impossible, walked out soon afterwards. To show his mother-in-law he was not in the least offended he wore a passable smile as he left the room.

'Titi, what do you think of your friend's attitude?' Wonuma began. 'Disgraceful isn't it? Don't you advise her? Maybe she would listen to you.'

'Ahule will be all right in the end I am sure,' Titi replied sagely.

'But when?'

'There is plenty of time. They have not done the formal wine carrying yet, have they?'

122

'That will be by the new moon which is at hand.'

Ekwueme on his side also puzzled over his bride's attitude. She must be a queer girl, he thought. Not that he cared very much. In fact he went about the marriage like a sleep-walker. But he could not help wondering, in an idle sort of way, what life with this capricious, energetic, over-shy young woman would be like.

The day for the formal 'presentation of wine' arrived. This time Wigwe was accompanied by several village elders. They were all neatly dressed in gay wrappers and sang their way to Omigwe. As they passed by, housewives peeped out with wistful looks in their eyes, their minds thrown back to the days when like Ahurole they waited anxiously for the wine party to arrive at their fathers' compounds.

Wine carrying was expensive on both sides. Wagbara with the help of his neighbours prepared a great feast for his guests and made sure that nothing was lacking. Not that he could not do it alone, but the neighbours could not bear to see him have all the fun of entertaining. Ahurole was their child too. They could not stay back on a great occasion like this. They bustled about swopping stories with their guests, many of them their personal friends.

Traditionally, Ahurole was to return the calabashes after this great occasion. She would stay in her husband's house for four days before returning to her parents. Accordingly Wonuma was very busy seeing to it that everything about her daughter was perfect. She got a neighbour to do a beautiful indigo design on her. This particular design was reserved for great occasions and involved long back-breaking sittings. The results justified the pains. With her ojongo hair style and rare beads (Wonuma had sought the bottom of her chests) many a man envied the bridegroom.

It was late when the marriage party trooped back to Omokachi. Adaku was fully prepared to welcome her prospective daughter-in-law and her train and had prepared a lot of food. But no one could taste her dishes; Wagbara had fed them with a lavishness bordering on the prodigious. A few die-hards tried but gave up after several heavy belches closely approaching regurgitation. Singing and dancing took up the rest of the night. Ekwueme did not sing but Mmam, Wakiri and other songsters excused him. It was a great night. Wigwe was happy and proud. Nothing revealed his happiness more than the brief dancing he did when Mmam, now twice a genius under the good influence of several blends of palm wine, beat the drum as he had never done before. The audience was thrilled and several neighbours presented Wigwe with money. It was worth doing for who knew when, if ever, he would dance again.

The next four days were not easy for Ahurole. All eyes were on her, all her movements watched. This was not a cruel concerted effort to find faults. Rather Ekwueme's relations were prejudiced in Ahurole's favour and they strove to justify their confidence in her by picking up and exaggerating every virtue she exhibited. She was petted, praised, and overfed. Kind words greeted her all round and she was happy. There is nothing that softens human nature as much as kindness and love. Surrounded by these, Ahurole's better nature predominated. Her unpredictable dispositions became passive and more controlled. Her spontaneous weeping sessions were forgotten. Her illogicalities vanished.

Prominent among the many villagers who came to pay calls on Ahurole were girls in her age-group. A noisy frolicsome bunch, they dropped in at all hours of the day. Ahurole was always available for, in spite of her protests, she was not allowed to go to the farm during her four-day stay at her husband's. She knew most of the girls; Omigwe shared much of its social life with Omokachi. The girls were for the most part amiable and eager to please her. They also tried hard to point out that she would settle down quickly. What was there anyway at Omigwe to make anyone nostalgic?

'You will find it difficult to visit your parents,' one girl said pointedly.

'Why?' Ahurole wondered.

'You will be too fond of our village.' Ahurole did her best to defend her village but what could she do against so many girls, some of them more spirited than she was?

'Our village is much bigger.'

'We grow bigger yams.'

'Our ponds yield much more fish.'

'Our wrestlers are unbeatable.' And so they went on reeling off the advantages of their beloved village. At first Ahurole was tense, but finding herself hopelessly overwhelmed she relaxed and listened passively with some amusement. Then someone said:

'And our young men are more handsome.' At this there was prolonged giggling.

'There you go with your brazen talk,' another girl tried to chide the first.

'But it is true, really true.'

'We know but why say it so openly?'

'Why not? Look at Ekwueme for instance.'

The giggling grew into a roar this time. Ahurole saw the irrefutable logic in this last statement and could not hold back a smile.

'Do not compel me to name some ugly men of Omokachi,' Ihuoma put in quietly. Being a daughter of Omigwe herself she was the only person trying to argue on Ahurole's side. Her defence was weakened by the fact that she often admitted with characteristic honesty any adverse arguments which rang indefensibly true. Again she didn't speak with quite as much heat as the younger girls.

She was glad to have made it at last. If she had not dropped in to see Ahurole during the four days' stay, such a gesture would have been capable of almost any interpretations. She was lucky too that she came at a time when Ekwueme was doing the rounds of his traps. It had not been an easy decision to make. But propriety in the village often outweighed personal emotional conflicts and she knew all along that she would have to pay the call.

Happy now that her son was being properly married, Adaku no longer bore any ill feelings towards Ihuoma. She greeted her very cordially when she arrived and inquired after her children. Wigwe found it harder to sham cordiality. When Ihuoma greeted him, he mumbled something and looked down. In this movement his face was replaced by a white shroud – his grey hairs. Looking at that, Ihuoma's resentment lessened considerably.

One by one the girls went away until only Ihuoma and Ahurole were left.

'You will find it nice here,' Ihuoma said.

'So the girls say.'

'You have married into a quiet, self-respecting family.'

'I think so.'

'Well, it is up to you to uphold the good name of our village. Remember that Omigwe girls have always made good wives anywhere.'

125

'That is true.'
'I am leaving now to do some weeding around my house. I shall see you again.'
'Thank you. You have done well.'

CHAPTER NINETEEN

Ihuoma left feeling immensely relieved. Things would be normal now – at least to all appearances. Whatever she felt was safely locked up in her mind. Not even her mother could probe into its depths and wrench its secrets. She had admitted to herself that she liked Ekwe very much. But what woman does not like some man? Her liking for Ekwe was not frantic nor was it sudden. It had grown gradually over a long period. Since it did not take her by storm she was able to keep it firmly under control.

Omokachi village life was noted for its tradition, propriety, and decorum. Excessive or fanatical feelings over anything were frowned upon and even described as crazy. Anyone who could not control his feelings was regarded as being unduly influenced by his agwu. Anyika often confirmed this, as in Ahurole's case.

Even love and sex were put in their proper place. If a woman could not marry one man she could always marry another. A woman deliberately scheming to land a man was unheard of. True, she might encourage him, but this encouragement was a subtle reflex action, a legacy of her prehistoric ancestors. A mature man's love was sincere, deep and stable and therefore easy to reciprocate, difficult to turn down. That was why it was possible for a girl to marry a man without formal courtship. Love was love and never failed.

That was Ihuoma's world and she behaved true to type. Ekwueme's father had played his part even if over-zealously; Ekwueme had been dutiful; Ahurole had turned out well; it was up to her to avoid behaving in a way that might disrupt this perfect setting. She had had her chance and if the gods had been rather cruel there was nothing she could do about it. She threw herself into the business of switching her mind from whatever had gone before. She worked with renewed energy on her farm, gave her children extra care and attention and danced on moonlit nights as happily as anybody else. She did not find it particularly difficult to talk freely to Ekwueme when they met.

'Ekwe.'

'Ihuoma.'

'Will you sing a new song tonight?'

'Yes, two in fact.'

'Which are they?'

'There is one about how Wodu Wakiri fell off a palm wine tree under the sting of bees.'

'How funny.'

'Very funny. Wakiri composed it himself.'

'What a rascal he is.'

'The other is about a man in Chiolu who tried to make love to a woman in the farm.'

'How terrible! He must have been bewitched.'

'Of course he was. He could not have done it in his right mind. In any case he is groaning under the highly involved purification rites.'

That was long enough and Ihuoma broke off to join others gossiping in groups on the arena. It was a dance night and the moon was just rising. Tonight it rose too late for supper. Wodu Wakiri arrived and the dance started. At first the singing was not firm. That was because they were learning the two songs recently composed. The learning period was rather prolonged because half the singers could not help laughing at the song Wakiri composed on himself. There were shouts of 'Wodu, you're a real clown!' 'Wodu, you are lost indeed.' 'Wodu, when will you grow up?' 'Ah, Wodu you will make us die of laughter.'

At last the singing and dancing warmed up and the anxious hips of girls vibrated in unison.

CHAPTER TWENTY

Six months after the start of negotiations, Ahurole was being escorted finally to her husband's house. It was a pace-making marriage. The normal period of negotiations was a year, but Wigwe
had rushed things. Each time Wagbara pointed out that a hen
cannot lay eggs and hatch them on the same day, Wigwe had
countered by saying that the slow-footed always fail in battle. And
so Ahurole was home in six months. Negotiations were not really
ended but Wigwe had done everything necessary to make it possible for his daughter-in-law to be led home. Whatever was left –
by no means negligible – could be taken in slower strides. The old
man breathed a sigh of relief.

Ahurole's bridal train was a train indeed. It carried all that went
to make the home of a young couple comfortable. Even goats,
chickens and a she-dog were included.

'Ahurole, you will wash my wrapper tomorrow,' Mmam the
drummer announced solemnly when they arrived.

'I shall, but why?' Ahurole asked.

'Your chickens have left some droppings on my wrapper.'

'Ewu! I am sorry,' she said.

'Well, I suppose you wouldn't object to the meat,' Wakiri
chuckled.

'The meat doesn't go with the droppings, or does it?' Mmam
replied with some heat.

'It might, you know.'

'You are mad.'

'Ever enjoyed the entrails of a chicken? I bet you never can
wash out all the droppings,' Wakiri said. Several members of the
bridal group grinned as they left for their homes.

Ekwueme had now reconciled himself to the marriage. Everyone approved of Ahurole. In the end he believed them. They could
not all be wrong. Ihuoma's image gradually sank into his sub-
conscious but after a hard struggle. Perhaps what made his
struggles easier was Ihuoma's attitude towards the whole thing. By
what seemed a miracle she recovered her former aplomb and

129

cheerfulness and now and then came into Wigwe's compound to chat with them. If she could show such indifference he certainly could do the same.

To his surprise Ekwueme found that his normal daily routine hardly changed now that he was married. He still inspected his traps at the usual time, went hunting when he wanted, sang in the dance arena on nights when the moon swept the ground. What was more, when he came home from the bush he still enjoyed the foo-foo left overnight in his mother's kitchen. This overnight foo-foo had a special flavour which nothing else seemed to match. Even the process of warming up the soup was a pleasure.

Often he wondered whether he was behaving as a married man should. He felt his mind was annoyingly boyish but there was nothing he could do about it. At one stage he decided to look as serious as possible. He moved about with a solemn air and wore a crease-tortured brow but he abandoned this pose under Wakiri's irrepressible sarcasm.

For the first few months Ahurole and her husband ate from the same plot with the rest of the family. Later she was ceremoniously installed in her own hearth. Then Ekwe felt he was truly married and played the man at every possible opportunity. He cut down on frivolous talk as much as possible and on his dancing.

'Look chaps, I am getting old,' he would declare at every opportunity to the great amusement of his friends. Though he had no child yet, he began to get into the habit of saying 'my son' when addressing a little child. At first he felt like an impostor and the words rolled out heavily from his mouth. To make it easier for himself he confined this practice to very small children to begin with. He improved on his stock of proverbs and practised saying them in a slow deliberate drawl with a chunk of kola delicately poised between his lips.

All this show of manliness notwithstanding, Ekwueme still enjoyed his mother's overnight foo-foo. He found this habit difficult to break.

Ahurole showed no resentments, at least not outwardly. What wife would ever try to stop a man from feeding in his mother's house? It would be the height of childish possessiveness. In any case this habit became a household joke and Ahurole shared it as best she could.

'I don't blame Ekwe,' Adaku would say, 'you see Nkechi my

130

second child was long in coming and Ekwe got used to the bottom of the pot.'

Ekwueme was indeed an only child for almost twelve years. Wigwe had despaired and was thinking of getting another wife when his wife became pregnant again and little Nkechi came into the world. During those twelve years Ekwueme had the attentions due to an only child. He was very well fed and grew rapidly. His mother guarded him jealously and did her best to discourage him from any activities that might hurt him. This annoyed Wigwe but what could he do; the child was more often than not in his mother's company.

In his early years Ekwe was often jeered at by his fellow boys because he was slow and clumsy and could not do many of the things which boys in his age group could do. He could not make thatches, he was poor with bows and arrows; he was well beaten in the few fights he was ever involved in; he could not wrestle. Each time he came home crying, Wigwe would try to send him back into the streets to fight it out, but Adaku's pleadings always prevailed. She was sure the child was not weak. It was because he was growing too fast. One day he would be able to beat back his assailants. Wigwe accused his wife of trying to make a woman out of a man. She in turn accused him of setting too high a standard for a very young child. She pointed out to Wigwe's amusement that at Ekwe's age he himself could not even walk, let alone talk of wrestling and fighting.

One day young Ekwe was pummelling it out with a young boy at the entrance to his father's compound. As usual he was having the rougher end of the deal. He decided to turn round and race for it. Then he saw his mother approaching and developed some courage. He gave his opponent a desperate push. Luck was on his side. The boy stumbled over a coconut branch with which they had been playing and fell heavily. Ekwe made faces at his victim by opening his eyes wide with his forefingers, then he raced home joyfully. His mother who had seen everything was there to receive him.

'There you are,' she said, 'I know you are strong and can beat any boy in your group dizzy, when you want to.' The story went round among the little boys and overnight Ekwueme's reputation rose. He was a chap to be reckoned with and youngsters ceased to bother him.

131

In order not to let his mother down, young Ekwe tried to be in the forefront of everything. He began wrestling seriously and though he was not very good his mates feared his tenacity and aggressiveness. He refused to pick and choose like others; he wrestled with anyone who wanted to. He surprised his father one day by volunteering to accompany him on his trapping round. This was a thing his mother had always prevented him from doing in spite of Wigwe's protests. Now he wanted to and waved aside his mother's objections angrily. His father was happy. He rummaged in his room and found a small sooty matchet.

'I used this when I was your age,' he said, 'now it is your turn to use it.'

They marched off into the forest and so began Ekwueme's hunting and trapping career.

Ekwueme grew to be good in many things. But all his efforts were directed towards pleasing his mother, to justify her confidence in him. He valued her praise more than anything else. His relationship with his father was cordial but he preferred his mother's company to his father's. He would sit in the kitchen with her after his trapping and watch her cook. He would chat with her for hours in the evening while his father dozed off by his lonely fire in the reception hall.

Compared to his mates Ekwueme was not keen on women. Oh yes, he could dash around with them in the arena and absorb any amount of slaps and scratches like any other young man but he never really felt excited by them. A lot of his energy went into his trapping and hunting and he always said he was too busy to fool around with women. They were childish anyway and not worth bothering about. The only woman he ever liked apart from his mother was Ihuoma. She was so understanding, motherly and beautiful. Ahurole was beautiful. He hoped she would be understanding and – perhaps motherly as well.

That first meal they had on their own hearth launched the young couple into the largely uncharted, if much sailed matrimonial sea. The meal was a success all right; it had to be. For one thing Adaku had carefully briefed her daughter-in-law on her son's likes and dislikes; for another Ahurole had a lot of meat and fish and ingredients to choose from. Her parents and her parents-in-law saw to that.

It was a rainy day and after the meal Ekwueme relaxed with his wife in their newly built kitchen. There was some fresh meat smoking over the fireplace and Ahurole sat near the fire to tend it. Her husband sat on a broad three-legged chair which he had made a few days ago. One could see it was new; the red sap of the wood still showed around the cut edges.

'This meat has much fat in it. It keeps the fire going as it drips into it,' Ahurole said, trying to keep the rising flames down.

'Wild hogs are always like that,' Ekwe said.

'Yes, I remember when my father used to kill them.'

'Did he ever kill any?'

'How can you ask? Is he not one of our greatest game killers?'

'Anyway, he killed just a few.'

'No, he killed several.'

'They were small ones.'

'How do you know?'

'You see hogs were not quite so large in those days.'

'What have you done to make them bigger?'

'Nothing. They have been growing up, that's all.'

'Are they full size now?'

'I don't know.'

'Why not? You claim to know much about their growth.' Several drops of fat dripped into the fire simultaneously and the flames flared up. Ahurole quickly removed a few sticks and the flames went down. She got up, sprinkled some water over the smoking faggots she had withdrawn from the fire and sat down again.

Outside it drizzled monotonously. There was no change in the intensity of the rain. The slight wind provided the only variation. It blew this way and then that, altering the course of the smoke from Ahurole's hearth. Twice Ekwueme changed his position to avoid the smoke. When it came his way the third time he refused to move and sat tight, sniffing and trying to breathe through the mouth.

'Why don't you change your position?' his wife asked.

'Because I have done it twice. I am not prepared to be chased from one corner to the other.'

'The smoke seems to like you.'

'I hope it will extend its love to you.'

'I know what to do.'

'What will you do?'

'Remove the particular faggot giving out the smoke.'

133

'Please do so,' Ekwueme said bending sideways to give his streaming eyes some fresh air. His wife removed a smoking fire brand and threw it into the rain. The smoke abated and changed direction, this time towards her.

'Ah, it is annoyed with me,' she said.

'No, it likes you,' her husband retorted.

'I shall drive it towards you again.'

'Let's see you do it.'

'I shall employ a charm I used to know when I was a child,' Ahurole said smiling.

'And what are you now?'

'An old woman, of course.'

'Fine. Go ahead with your charm, anyway.'

Ahurole cleared her throat. 'You see,' she said, 'it is in the form of a song.'

'Go on,' Ekwueme urged. She half sang, half said the incantation.

'Smoke go, go away,
Smoke go, go away,
I haven't got your broken pot,
Ekwe has your broken pot;
Smoke please go to him.'

'That is exactly what my little sister does when the smoke worries her,' Ekwueme said.

'Quite true, most children know the song.'

'But there are slight variations from village to village.' The smoke was on Ekwueme again.

'There you are,' his wife said triumphantly. This time her husband changed his position.

'Ekwe, eh . . . my lord, what will you have for supper?'

'Anything.'

'Would yam porridge do?'

'Anything, I said.'

'I just want to make sure I prepare what you want.'

'You ought to know by now. Will you ask me before every meal?'

'My lord, we have just started cooking on our own.'

'You were with my mother for a couple of months.'

'But then your mother cooked according to your father's appetite.'

134

'My father's appetite is mine.'

'I shall prepare yam porridge then?'

'If you like.'

'My lord, why not tell me?'

'You must learn to use your discretion as from now.'

'Ekwe! Ekwe! Come and take!' Adaku yelled from the other side of the compound. Ekwueme moved over to see what it was. He came back to find his wife in tears.

'What is it, Ahule?' he asked baffled and rather irritated. For answer his wife wiped one eye after the other with a corner of her wrapper.

'What is it?'

Ahurole raised her face and gazed rigidly at a point far beyond the compound.

'So this little discussion over food is sufficient to make you cry, is it? I should never correct you, is that it? Look, such an attitude is childish. You are a wife not a baby, you must learn to take things accordingly.'

With that Ekwueme strode into his room and lay on his bed. This was the most disagreeable thing about Ahurole, crying over nothing. Otherwise, he thought, she was doing well. What irritated him most was that any time she had this crying fit, she would sulk until he calmed her as he would a baby. He hated having to soothe anyone. He remembered when he used to beat his little sister Nkechi. He never could bring himself to soothe her afterwards.

His room grew dark and he found his mother standing by the door.

'What has happened?' she asked.

'Where?'

'What is wrong with Ahurole?'

'Let her tell you.'

'She refused to tell me.'

'I can't tell you either.'

'Ekwe don't keep things to yourself. Why not . . .'

Ekwe sprang up and faced his mother.

'Look, why does she carry on like that?'

'How?'

'Why does she cry for no reason?'

'Was there no quarrel?'

'None.'

Adaku thought for a while.

'You see, Ekwe, she is young and does not quite understand herself. She will stop it after a time. Go and be nice to her. She will stop sulking.'

'No, that would merely encourage her to be silly.'

'No, it wouldn't.'

'You seem to feel I am to blame. I tell you I did not even abuse her. Why should I plead with her over nothing?'

'I know, Ekwe, but do as I tell you.'

'All right, I shall think about it.'

'No, no, go right now, my son.'

She placed her right arm round her son and took him over to her daughter-in-law. Then she withdrew. Ahurole's eyes were still red and her chest heaved. Ekwueme looked at her hard and long, let out a deep sigh and went to her.

'Stop crying now,' he said, 'there is really no need to. Stop crying, Ahule. I merely said you should use your discretion over meals. Was that an unheard-of thing?'

'It was the way you said it that annoyed me. You made me feel very foolish.'

CHAPTER TWENTY-ONE

It did not take Ekwueme long to know what he was up against in his marriage. His wife was good – good for an old man that is. An old man who would pet her all day long and endure her sudden and apparently unprovoked floods of tears. For a young man she was trying.

When she was not sulking, Ahurole was vivacious and full of pranks. She would wrestle energetically in the bedroom with her husband amidst tumbling chairs, laughing happily. But when her tears set in, she presented an alarmingly contrasting picture.

All the efforts of her parents to tame her agwu were largely wasted. Anyika had not been at his best. Ekwueme and his mother consulted him again and he did what he could but warned them that Ahurole's agwu would never be completely overcome.

Ekwueme's reaction was to avoid quarrelling as much as possible. He would joke with her within a certain safe limit. As soon as he noticed any signs of discontent or sulks he would move off to see Wakiri or to inspect a near trap. Often he succeeded in warding off unpleasant scenes. When he failed he faced days of red-eyed pouting.

At first Adaku blamed her son for the constant quarrels. She claimed:

'A young wife has the right to "make faces" in her first few months of marriage, because that is the time she enjoys her husband most. When the babies arrive and maybe other wives join her it becomes too late.' Later she wasn't quite sure whom to blame. Later still she began to give Ahurole serious private lectures.

'My daughter,' she said, 'you must remember that you are a woman now – you will have a baby. Whose tears would we heed, yours or the baby's?'

'Nne, maybe I cry more than is necessary but your son is always to blame. He is fond of scolding. When he is not scolding his voice is harsh and menacing.'

'But that is the way of men. He is usually not as angry as he may look. He has not given you a beating yet, has he?'

137

'No, but I prefer a beating to severe scolding.'

'Does he scold you all that much?'

'He does.'

'All right, I shall see that he stops it. Meanwhile remember that you are grown up.'

Ekwueme himself endured a few lectures from his mother and he did his best to take her advice. For all that, the domestic tension was not lessened. Ahurole expected far more gentleness than her husband could give. On the other hand Ekwueme's ideal wife was a composed stable woman who could get on without too much help from him. More, he wanted a woman who would not only receive praise and encouragement but also give them in return; a mature woman, soothing and loving. A woman who would act for him in an emergency if he were away. A woman . . . a woman . . . well, something like his mother. Not quite though, because Adaku could get terribly angry with his father once in a while. No, he couldn't face that in his wife.

Wigwe did not offer his son any advice. He felt he would in time learn his own lessons and adjust. Why, he used to quarrel almost every day with Adaku in their first years of marriage. Those fights. They were interesting now that he was reviewing them through the softening vista of years. With amused fascination he watched his son's domestic struggles. He could tell when he was happy or sad, when a quarrel was brewing or had been made up. He was pleased to see the manly determination on his son's face to bear his troubles calmly and live like any other married man. But gradually this determination turned to indifference. He could see that clearly. The way he handled his matchet when going trapping, his rather noisy laughter, his enhanced interest in singing and dancing all showed it. Indifference was not a good thing in marriage, and Wigwe sought an opportunity to speak to his son. He did not want to make it a parental lecture. An informal chat would do more good, he thought. His chance came one evening when Ekwueme was returning from a dance. It was rather late and only a few old men were still outside warming themselves by the fire in their reception halls.

'Ekwe, I thought the dance was to have lasted all night,' Wigwe said.

'Yes father, but Mmam complained that his male drum was not in order and forced us home.'

'What was wrong with it?'

'There was a hole in the skin and the tear grew worse as the dance progressed.'

'I thought a new skin was put on a few months ago.'

'Under Mmam's fingers, no skin can really last.' His father chuckled.

'Didn't your wife attend the dance?'

'No, father, she was too busy making faces.'

'Over what?'

'Over nothing as usual.'

'Ekwe, listen. You must know that the beginning of a marriage is not easy. In my first year of marriage I quarrelled so much with your mother that people thought the marriage would not stick. Here we are after some thirty years.'

'You can't compare mother to that agwu-troubled baby of mine. Mother is far more mature. She is . . .'

'Now, yes, but not then.'

'Ahurole is a unique type of woman altogether.'

'Now, my son, all women are the same. Ahurole will learn as the years go by. But what you must never dò is to turn your back on her. If you do she will never learn your ways nor you hers. Also it is no use getting very hot each time you quarrel. Think of her as a baby needing constant correction. When a baby annoys you, you don't carry the anger with you all day, do you? Treat your wife the same. After all, you are several years older than she is.'

'If only she could give reasons for her crying.'

'Why bother? She doesn't cry with your eyes does she? Your eyes will not redden and swell, hers will. When you find her crying don't get angry. If you can, get out of the house and let her empty her pond of tears. When she's done she'll be the wiser and calmer for it.'

'I still think her agwu is worrying her. Look, father, there are other young married women of her age. Why don't they cry and make faces so much?'

Wigwe wanted to tell his son that it was partly his fault; that he was trying to make a mother of his wife; but he found no proverb subtle enough to convey the message home.

'Ahurole may be of the crying type, but she should change if you follow my advice. Go to bed, my son. May the day break.'

'May the day break, father.'

Full of thought Ekwueme went to bed. He did not sleep until partridges began to laugh in the near-by bushes. He turned his father's words over and over again in his mind but he did not quite see his fault. Many men beat their wives; he hadn't done so yet. Others exchanged bitter words for long hours with their wives; he avoided talking as much as possible. Meat was in constant supply. She was not lacking in wrappers. No, the girl was abnormal and he unlucky to have married her. Often he compared his mother to Ahurole and each time his wife fell far short of expectations. Ahurole was little better than his sister Nkechi. He wondered how she would ever manage children of her own.

Surely all the young married girls were not like this? Mentally he reeled off a couple of names. They were all excellent girls playing their role apparently with inborn ease. Bad luck, sheer bad luck to have married Ahurole. No one could blame him. That was what came of a childhood engagement. Otherwise he might have married any of the other girls. He focused his attention on some of the young married girls. Strangely, none appealed to him forcibly. Now that he examined them critically he found things he did not like in every one of them. He turned over on his belly and a wave of hatred for all young girls swept through him. They were stupid, horrible. He had always held that view and now by his marriage he was proved right. All his determination to mould Ahurole into a mature woman melted. He felt beaten. His indifference changed into resignation. Ahurole was an unhappy load on his head and he just had to carry it.

His unhappiness was heightened by the fact that no one seemed to understand his problem. Even his parents who should know better were indirectly heaping a disproportionate share of the blame on him. He dared not confide in Wakiri and his other friends. They would merely laugh. Surrounded as he was by parents, relations and friends, the feeling of loneliness was unnerving. To relieve his overburdened mind and court sleep he began to reconstruct his image of an ideal wife. Like rain after a long dry season, her image came into his mind. She came with overwhelming tenderness and understanding in her eyes. The usual smile played on her lips, the gap in the teeth enhancing its innocent effect. The well formed limbs, the rounded buttocks all came in bold relief. With a cry he clutched the air and gasped 'Ihuoma!' Later he fell asleep.

140

'Ekwe, Ekwe, get up, my son.'

Ekwueme opened one eye and strong red shafts of sunlight from the roof pierced them. He jumped out of his bed and opened the door. His father was there to greet him.

'You are unusually late today, Ekwe.'

'I didn't sleep in time.'

'That is true. The dance kept you up.'

He confirmed his father's opinions and did not bother to add that his thoughts kept him awake most of the night.

He washed his hands, feet and face, stuck a chew-stick in his mouth, and strode away into the forest. When he came back in the evening his face still wore a depressed look. Ahurole, uneasy, stopped pouting.

'Let me have a warm bath,' he said.

'It is not quite ready, Ekwe,' said she.

'Why not?'

'The water cooled down when I took it off the fire to warm the soup for the evening meal. It will heat up quickly again.'

Ekwueme strolled off to his mother's kitchen to chat with his mother. When he came back his bath was not ready.

'I thought you went to bathe at your mother's,' Ahurole explained.

'How many times have I had my bath at my mother's?'

'I don't count. You can't blame me. You ought to have sat down in your house to rest and wait for your bath. Why can't you stay in your own kitchen?'

Ekwueme turned back abruptly and went into his room. He lay on his sleeping mound breathing deeply. Presently his wife came to announce that his bath was ready. He rose slowly cat-like and followed her.

He could not eat much that night. He had been very hungry when he came back from his trapping. Now somehow his stomach seemed full and his mind too.

'You haven't eaten much,' his wife observed.

'No, I am not that hungry.'

'I wish you had said so earlier. I put in much soup for you thinking you were very hungry.'

'You can have your soup. I didn't drink it all.'

'You don't expect me to pour that back into the pot, do you?'

'Do what you like, Ahurole. Just leave me alone.'

Before she went to bed, Ahurole went to check whether her husband's bed was in order. She found him eating groundnuts and dry corn.

'Ah, you said you were not hungry.'

'Yes, I did say that,' Ekwueme said raising his eyebrows.

'And what are you doing now?'

'Eating corn. Are you blind?'

'Why not say you don't like my cooking?' Ahurole pressed on.

'I may have no appetite for foo-foo and yet be able to eat corn, don't you see?'

'You don't like my cooking, that's all.'

'All right, I don't, but leave me alone.'

'Why did you not say so before? I could have got you some food from your mother's house.'

'Ahurole! Is your agwu on the warpath again?'

'Ekwe, what will I do to please you? Chei, chei, I am unfortunate in my marriage.' Her tears flowed fast.

For a time her husband halted his chewing and gaped at her open-mouthed. Then he resumed his methodical crushing of the dry corn grains. He sat with one leg stretched on the ground and the other resting on the chair on which he sat. He threw the corn grains into his mouth one by one and there was a resounding report as each one exploded between his strong molars. Ahurole stood by the door sobbing.

Suddenly Ekwe got up and ordered her to get off in an awful voice. Before she could move he gave her several slaps on the face and pushed her back violently. Ahurole fell flat on her back but sprang up with youthful elasticity and charged blindly at her husband.

'You will kill me today. You must kill me today,' she cried, 'and carry my body to my parents.'

Ekwueme shook her off and went in search of a cane. He came back brandishing a thick one but his parents intervened. He struggled to get at Ahurole but Wigwe held him fast. Adaku led Ahurole back to her room. Ekwueme offered no explanations. He felt he was about to burst. He struggled free, ran into his room and locked his door.

•

When Ekwueme returned from the bush the next day an empty

house stared at him. Ahurole was nowhere to be found. He thought she had gone off to fetch water or something. But there was no fire on the hearth, no sign of any activity.

'Mother, do you know where Ahurole is?'

'No, is she not around?'

'I can't find her. I have a feeling she has run away.'

'Let us wait for a while,' Adaku said uneasily.

'Mother, I saw her tying up her clothes into a bundle,' Nkechi cut in. 'When I questioned her she said she was going to the well to wash them.'

'Run to the well and see if she is there,' Ekwueme said.

'Go and tell your father that Ahurole is missing,' Adaku said.

'Nothing to worry about,' Wigwe said from the reception hall. 'Ekwe, go to Omigwe and find out if she is staying with her parents.'

Ekwueme collected a calabash of palm wine and set out reluctantly. When he arrived at his in-law's he was duly informed that Ahurole was with them.

'Of course you can't take her away today,' Wagbara said, 'You will come on the third day for a settlement according to custom.'

Their statements before their parents were essentially the same; there were few contradictions. The young couple were praised for their truthfulness. Said Wigwe:

'This clearly shows that each of them is interested in the marriage.'

What surprised even the couple themselves was the realization that they had been quarrelling over nothing. Ahurole discovered she had practically no excuse for crying her head off. Ekwueme thought it was childish of him to have been unduly disturbed by Ahurole's crying. All the old men agreed that nothing serious was involved in the quarrel. They drank Ekwueme's palm wine and dispersed.

Ekwueme was annoyed with himself. Before marriage he thought he knew all the answers to domestic problems and vowed that when he got married he would never have to call in a third party, not even his parents, to decide anything between him and his wife. He used to despise men who had to beat their wives and call in arbitrators to settle disputes every other day. Now that he was one of them, he felt confused.

When the old men were analysing their quarrels, everything had

143

looked simple. Ekwueme had come back with his wife confident that he could now cope with the situation. But the very next day they were back where they started. His resentment and resignation deepened. He tried to ignore his wife as much as possible. In retaliation she avoided him. They spoke to each other in monosyllables and only on inevitable topics like eating. Gradually the gulf widened between them.

CHAPTER TWENTY-TWO

The sun was making its way towards Chiolu and yet the waterside market was littered with unsold yams. The Rikwos, the principal customers, were strolling idly from one yam mound to another offering provocative prices for magnificent yams. Women piled abuses on them, calling them an indolent lot who could only manage canoes but could not tell whether yams grew in the air or underground. But the Rikwos were experts in this battle of nerves. They knew that in time the yam sellers would beg them to buy. Otherwise how could they carry their heavy loads back to the village? Sure enough soon exhausted men and women who had several heaps of yam were forced to sell them at give-away prices. Worse still, they had to help the Rikwos carry the yams into their boats by the riverside. Why couldn't the fools carry the yams themselves many a youth often asked. Older people told them it was an unfortunate tradition. They could not break it without a serious crisis.

One would think fish would be cheap too. Far from it. The crafty Rikwos had a strong trade union and demanded extortionate prices for their fish. It was all very unfair. Everyone, except the Rikwos of course, agreed it was a bad market day.

Disappointed groups of people made their way along the narrow path to the village chatting about the ever-falling prices for their farm produce. There were young women hurrying home to prepare the evening meal, young men walking at a slow pace and teasing the impatient women, taciturn old bachelors and widowers clutching their baskets. One group contained Otudo the madman. He was brushing past people rapidly as if pressed for time. Villagers were used to him. They knew he would walk back again to the market where he normally stayed. He usually went back at dusk. Saying that one met Otudo on his way back was another way of stating that one came back very late from the market.

Each group grew longer as it progressed and stragglers from one group merged with the next group behind. Ekwueme was one of the stragglers. Like most people that day the market had offered

145

him little but that was not what occupied his thoughts. He was thinking of nothing in particular. But his mind was not blank either. A vague oppressive blanket of sadness enveloped him as he walked along slowly. He did not notice the impatient folks streaming past him. One or two tried to engage him in conversation. They pushed past him when he did not reciprocate. Presently a familiar voice called him. He looked sideways and found Ihuoma walking by his side.

'Ihuoma, welcome. How was the day?' he asked.

'This is all I have for twenty prize yams,' Ihuoma said, jingling a few manillas tied to one corner of her wrapper.

'It is so with everyone. The Rikwos are becoming intolerable.'

'You know what is wrong with us?'

'No.'

'We can't make rules and stick to them.'

'What rules?' Ekwueme asked.

'Rules on the sale of yams.'

'No rules will work.'

'Because we are greedy.'

'You are right.'

'You remember one market day we decided not to carry any yams to the market. Well, didn't some poor fellows sell yams to the Rikwos?'

'Quite a number did,' Ekwe said chuckling, 'Oh, it was so funny. The first man who was seen on his way said the yams were meant for a relation of his living with the Rikwos. The second man said he was storing his yams at the market place for sale on the next market day. A third gave an even funnier excuse. In the end half the village were hauling yams to the market.'

Ihuoma laughed in her quiet way. She had been walking without holding her basket. Now as her head and shoulders shook with laughter she was obliged to grip her basket to prevent it from falling. Ekwueme did not laugh but somehow her laughter made him happy. He felt more relaxed and his burden of unhappiness eased off somewhat. He walked more jauntily now, Ihuoma setting the pace. Where the path was wide they walked side by side, and where narrow Ekwueme kept behind. He found himself talking easily, jokingly, and his companion laughed. How pleasant it was to watch her laugh, he thought. Sometimes when a joke was particularly funny Ihuoma turned back to look at him in mock re-

146

proach. Ekwueme would smile broadly and return the glance.

'I shall not sell any yams at the next market,' Ihuoma announced.

'Why?'

'They sell so cheap and my yams are so few that I cannot afford to throw them away like that.'

'What will you take to the market?'

'Cocoyams.'

'Your cocoyams should do well this year.'

'How do you know?'

'I have seen your cocoyam plot.'

'Where is it?'

'Near that big silk cotton tree.'

'You are right.'

'Have you harvested them already?'

'No, I shall be doing so for the next three days.'

'It is not a bad idea,' Ekwueme said; 'just now cocoyams are best sellers, particularly the reddish type. The lazy Rikwos scramble for them.'

'You know one thing?'

'What?'

'The Rikwos eat the very best of our products. All the big yams and cocoyams go to them. We the producers are content with the very worst.'

'That is true. On the other hand we eat the best fish. They make do with periwinkles and clams.'

'But we eat periwinkles too. I have some in my basket right now.'

'Yes, and I can also see the tail of what must be a very big fish.'

'You have sharp eyes, Ekwe.'

'A hunter should.'

'How are your traps?'

'As productive as usual.'

'What was the last big game you caught?'

'A big wild hog.'

'Difficult to dry because of the fat.'

'Yes, my . . . my wife complained it was dripping fat all over the place.'

'How is Ahurole? I am sorry I haven't called on her for so long.'

147

'Try and call on her and see if you can advise her too.'

'Advise her?'

'Yes, advise her.'

Ihuoma sensed what was coming. Like every other villager, she knew about Ekwueme's quarrels with his wife. She would very much have liked to advise Ahurole, particularly as they were both from the same village, but past events made it impossible for her to do so. She knew that Ekwueme's feelings for her were as strong as ever and she tried to avoid arousing them. How could she who was reputed to be one of the best women in Omokachi sow the seeds of confusion between a young man and his wife? She would rather die than be branded a husband-snatcher. It was too disgusting for words. If she changed the subject abruptly it would be as bad as pursuing it deeply. She went on cautiously:

'Ahurole will learn in time. Every young wife quarrels with her husband violently to begin with.'

'You don't know your village girl.'

'I do.'

'Advise her?'

'She needs no advice.'

Ekwueme faced her suddenly.

'Look Ihuoma, why this pretence? It is unlike you. Ahurole is impossible, why not admit it? Since I married her, life has not been the same. I am miserable, don't you see?'

Ihuoma was frightened. She didn't know how to get out of this. She blamed herself for inquiring after Ahurole and yet it was only proper that she should. She thought quickly but found no adequate reply. So she kept quiet not even daring to cough. She dreaded this explosion because she knew instinctively that Ekwueme was near breaking point. She knew that he was like an animal at bay looking for a way out. If she allowed him to pour his soul out to her, a sixth sense told her that it would not stop there. Lacking a spur, Ekwueme maintained a sullen silence. Ihuoma could hear his light footsteps coming resolutely behind her. She started shivering. She missed a step and nearly stumbled. As her uneasiness mounted, she dropped something and stopped to pick it up. Meanwhile she made way for her companion to pass, and breathed more easily. The sight of the first compound of the village reassured her.

Ihuoma's cocoyam plot was not far from the village. It was 'a home farm' as opposed to farms farther afield. It lay on one side of the path leading to the main farming area of the village. It was a hot afternoon but pear trees, palm wine trees and silk cotton trees provided adequate shade. That was a distinct advantage of a 'home farm'; it never lacked shady trees.

Ihuoma was harvesting her cocoyams alone. To fill up the silence she whistled and sang in turns. The whistling represented the music of the xylophone and her singing the normal rejoinder of dancers. By doing this double operation she lulled herself into the feeling of being in a dance arena and her loneliness vanished.

As she worked, passers-by greeted her and each time she stopped her work to reply. Occasionally she straightened up to exchange a few words with a neighbour.

'Ihuoma, are you working?' The woman looked up and saw Ekwueme passing by.

'Ekwe, are you off to the farm?'

'No, I want to inspect a trap near by. Are your cocoyams doing well?'

'Very well indeed. This particular plot has always been productive.'

'Let me have a look.' Ekwueme left the path and walked to where Ihuoma was.

'A rich harvest indeed,' he exclaimed.

'Yes, even more than I expected,' Ihuoma replied, beaming.

'The Rikwos will tear your basket from your head when you get to the market.'

'They will, and I shall bluff, if only to make up for their insolence of yesterday.'

'You are saying this for fun. You know you can't bluff.'

'I can and do at times.'

'Not you, Ihuoma.'

'Then I shall start it on the next market day.'

'You can't learn to be left-handed in old age, Ihuoma.'

'I am not old yet.'

'Of course not, that's how the saying goes.'

'Actually I am.'

'All right, you are,' said Ekwueme grinning. Ihuoma looked up at him and laughed lightly. Ekwueme moved nearer her and sat on an old fallen tree-trunk. He raised his matchet, buried its sharp blade in the bark of the tree and left it there quivering.

'You said you were going to inspect your traps?'

'Yes, but I am not in a hurry.'

'You should be. While you are here an animal can make good its escape.'

'My traps are escape-proof.'

'That is impossible, Ekwe.'

'Why?'

'Simply because no rope is that strong.'

'You don't know anything about traps, do you?'

'No, but I have seen one or two.'

'And you feel that has made you a trapper?'

'A woman can't be a trapper.'

'Good, so believe whatever I tell you about traps.'

'All right, but don't tell me lies.'

'I could lie to anyone but you.'

Ekwueme made this pronouncement rather solemnly but Ihuoma tried to make light of it.

'I tell you some animals are this very moment struggling free. Get going,' she said. But Ekwueme sat on conversing with her. He did not leave until Ihuoma announced that she was about to go, which was rather earlier than she would have done otherwise.

Ekwueme had no traps to inspect. But to keep up appearances he disappeared down an old track with a few disused traps. He hovered around for a while to give Ihuoma time to move away and then went home. His mind was relaxed and he felt happier than he had been for days.

The next day Ihuoma continued her harvest. A little way off lay an enviable pile of cocoyams, the result of her labours the day before. Another little heap grew as she flung cocoyams at it. She reckoned she would end up with at least three times four hundred large cocoyams.

'Ihuoma, you are still harvesting?'

She looked up and saw Nnenda by the path. 'Yes, I am.'

'Is the harvest good?'

'Very good, my sister. Just step over and have a look.' Nnenda came nearer and shouted in surprise. 'No one can beat you this year in cocoyams.'

Shortly afterwards the two women heard footsteps by the path. It was Ekwueme sauntering along matchet in hand. He lingered opposite the women for a while, exchanged a few words and

150

passed on. When Nnenda left, Ekwueme came back. He sat on the tree-trunk that had served him the previous day. But Ihuoma was more taciturn today. She worked furiously and it didn't take long before the silk cotton tree came between her and Ekwueme. Conversation became impossible and Ekwueme took his leave.

Ihuoma went home feeling worried. She had hoped that Ekwueme would in time forget about her. It now looked as if she was mistaken. She saw clearly that he was letting himself go and racked her brain for a way to keep him off. She was dismayed to find Ekwueme by her side at the cocoyam farm the next day. She thought of the number of passers-by who had seen them together during the past two days and her heart sank. In her desperation she found her tongue.

'Ekwe,' she said, 'why do you keep coming here? I am sure you are aware of the impression you are creating.'

'You are too particular, Ihuoma. What is wrong with us chatting together here?'

'You are bringing ridicule on me.'

'You are above any form of ridicule, Ihuoma.'

'You are married to my village girl. If she gets the impression that you are over-interested in me she will tell her parents and what type of figure will I cut at Omigwe?' Ekwueme was silent. He was cutting a pattern on the tree trunk with his matchet.

'Ekwe, please go away,' Ihuoma insisted. 'Go, go, please go.'

Adaku came by and Ekwe just managed to hide away. She greeted Ihuoma and passed.

'Now you see what I mean,' Ihuoma said when Ekwueme emerged once again.

'I do, but you realize I like you very much. I am sorry I am placing you in a difficult position but I don't mean any harm. Apart from my mother you are the only woman I really enjoy talking to. Why should you bother about what people say? We ourselves know that there is no undue intimacy between us.'

'Yes, but the neighbours don't know about that. They judge from what they observe. I don't mind if we chat at home but for you to come here persistently under the observation of passers-by is to invite the worst scandal imaginable.'

When Ekwueme eventually left, Ihuoma occupied his seat on the fallen tree and thought for some time. Her first impulse was to report the matter to Ekwueme's father. This would save her from any future complications, but it would humiliate Ekwe and she didn't want that. She thought of telling her mother to talk to Ekwueme but recalled that she rather liked him. Baffled, she resumed her work. She heaped the cocoyams in lots of four hundred, covered them with plantain leaves and went home.

The next day was a Great Eke. Ihuoma sat conversing with Nnenda in her reception hall.

'Nnenda, you will do me a favour?'

'I should be pleased,' Nnenda replied.

'I want you to speak to Ekwe on my behalf.'

'Have you offended him?'

'No. He is still pestering me. It will lead to no good. Ahurole is my village girl. Why should I come between her and Ekwueme? Besides I can't bear to be the subject of any unpleasant gossip in this village. I have told him I can't marry him. I can't be his mistress either. The matter should end there. Tell him that, please.'

'I see,' Nnenda said with some deliberation, 'you are quite right. I must say, however, I haven't seen him much with you. Do you think he deserves to be told off just now? Isn't he being just friendly as of old?'

'Nnenda, my sister, you are a woman as I am. We don't often make mistakes as regards men's feelings, do we? Ekwueme's advances, though not very frequent, are very serious. He almost frightens me. Do you know that in the last three days he has been coming to chat with me at the farm?'

'No indeed.'

'Well, you now see what I mean. Worse still he has not been getting on well with his wife. People will heap blame on me on the least suspicion. Then I think I should die.'

'Don't talk so, my sister. I will speak to him.'

'Make him realize that I do not hate him. Indeed he ought to have realized that by now. Tell him I respect and admire him but that anything beyond that will bring shame on us both.'

'I will do that,' Nnenda said, supporting her chin in her left palm. Evidently she was sharing her friend's embarrassment to the full.

'Or do you think I am being unduly stern?' Ihuoma asked, those tiny creases appearing on her brow.

'At first I thought so,' Nnenda said.

152

'I am wondering whether I can't hold him at bay by keeping strict watch on my words and actions. You see, I seem to feel it would be unfair to tell him off so roughly when in fact he has not done anything really wrong.'

Nnenda watched her friend keenly. For the first time, as far as she could remember, Ihuoma was not mistress of her feelings. Her indecision showed her confused state of mind and from the depths of her heart Nnenda felt an overwhelming sympathy for her young widowed friend. As her nearest neighbour she had watched her struggles against loneliness, against the advances of men. All along she had won and the respect which she commanded was something to be envied.

As her prestige mounted its maintenance became more trying. She became more sensitive to criticism and would go to any lengths to avoid it. The women adored her. Men were awestruck before her. She was becoming something of a phenomenon. But she alone knew her internal struggles. She knew she was not better than anyone else. She thought her virtues were the products of chance. As the days went by she began to loathe her so-called good manners. She became less delighted when people praised her. It was as if they were confining her to an ever-narrowing prison.

CHAPTER TWENTY-THREE

A goat can become an important member of a family. Ahurole's goat was a big brown she-goat which her mother had given her as a wedding present. At home at Omigwe Ahurole had fed it and driven it indoors on many a night. It was an old friend and she was doubly pleased when her mother gave it to her. Everyone in Wigwe's compound agreed it was a peculiar goat. For one thing it would not eat yams, but in compensation it had a double appetite for cassava. As yams were far more valuable than cassava this was a most welcome characteristic. For another, it had very short stout legs and never took long walks. It was always around the compound. The fireplace in the reception hall was its favourite resting-place. When there was no fire, it would push aside the half-burnt faggots and settle on the warm hearth to chew the cud. Perhaps the most important thing about this animal was its reproductive ability. It normally produced five kids at a time and right now its abdomen was greatly distended.

On this particular evening it was not about. Ahurole was the first to take notice and she duly informed her husband. With the lazy optimism of most husbands he dismissed her anxiety.

'Must be around somewhere,' he said and continued to chat with his father in the reception hall. After supper the goat had still not returned. Fearing a quarrel Ekwueme set out to look for it. The bright moonlight had fooled the animal, he thought, as he made his way from one compound to another making inquiries from neighbours.

Half-way through his search he entered Ihuoma's compound. She was indoors with her children. A beam of light struggled through a chink in the one-piece wooden door. Ekwueme looked around the compound before knocking at her door. She opened it enough to reveal her head.

'No,' she said, 'all the goats in here are mine.'

'Did you see this animal at any time during the day? Ekwueme asked.

'I can't tell since I don't know it.'

154

'It is big with unusually short legs. Colour mostly brown.'

'I don't remember seeing a goat like that.'

'I wonder where else to search.'

'Have you tried the other compounds?'

'I have tried most of them.'

'I am sorry, Ekwe, it must be the moonlight that is turning the poor animal's head.'

'Very bright, isn't it?'

'Very bright.'

'Ideal for a dance.'

'Quite true.' The man lingered for a while.

'May the day break,' Ihuoma broke the silence.

'May it break,' Ekwueme replied and turned to go as Ihuoma closed her door.

At the entrance to Ihuoma's compound Ekwueme met his wife. He was quite taken by surprise.

'What are you doing here?' he demanded.

'And what were you doing there?'

'Where?'

'At that woman's house.'

'Looking for the goat, what else?'

'Inside her house?'

'What are you talking about?'

'I saw when you came out and she locked the door.'

'Have you gone crazy?'

'Ekwe, you can't deny it. In any case, people have told me a great deal about your goings-on with this woman. You even pester her in her farm. Now, thank God, the stories have been confirmed before my own eyes.'

Ekwueme swallowed hard and strode away. He entered his room quietly and locked his door. He could hear his wife muttering.

'Just as I thought. He went off to have a good time with that stupid woman. No thought for our goat. I just wonder why people who are not ready for marriage take it on. Even a child can't behave this way . . .' Ekwueme turned this way and that on his bed while his wife spoke her mind in the next room. Unable to bear it any longer, he got up, locked the door and strolled out. A few people were still about, among them Wakiri, whose door was ajar, and Ekwueme knocked.

'Who is that?' Wakiri asked.

'Don't you know my voice, you ruffian?'

'Ah, Ada, do come in; I have been expecting you!'

'As if you have a lady-friend,' Ekwueme said bursting in.

'Ah, it is only you, Ekwe. I thought my girl friend Ada had come round to warm me up.'

'Shut up, you old pretender.'

'Sit down, Ekwedike,' Wakiri said adding a favourite suffix of his to Ekwe's name. Ekwueme unhooked a three-legged chair from the framework of the roof and sat down.

'The moon is full, Ekwe, I wish we were at the arena.'

'So do I.'

'By the way, before I talk nonsense, have you come for anything important?'

'No, Wakiri, my friend.' Ekwe loaded the last two words with sadness.

'But you are sad,' Wakiri insisted.

'Yes, I am.'

'What is it?'

'The old trouble.'

'Ahurole?'

'What else?'

'Take it coolly, my friend. You know, when it comes to nagging, I treat all women as children. If only you would do the same.'

'A wife's nagging can drive one crazy, it is very unlike a mother's nagging.'

Wakiri did not know what comfort to offer his friend. He was always at his wits' end when faced with deep sorrow. He himself made a joke of all his misfortunes and couldn't understand why people allowed themselves to become sad and depressed.

Presently an idea struck him. He dived under his bamboo bed and produced two small okwos made from Indian bamboo. He dived again and fished out a couple of drumsticks. Beating the time, he looked straight at his friend. It was a reassuring look, an invitation to forget his sorrows in music. Ekwueme stared back at him tongue-tied. But when Wakiri started he joined in. They sang about incidents in the town, about the rich and the poor, about sorrow and death. They mocked the headache of married life, they deplored the futility of life itself. Their singing filled the whole

156

compound but it did not disturb the occupants; it lulled them to sleep. Ekwueme's singing became rather frenzied. He shook his head as he sang and his looks were far away. Wakiri looked away when he saw tears running down his friend's cheeks.

*

The next day Ahurole was on her way to Omigwe to see her parents. Her husband who was lying at home with a headache had merely grunted when she had asked for his permission. She had interpreted the grunt positively and set out.

Her mother ran out to embrace her. Wagbara was attending a meeting of the elders, so mother and daughter had ample oppor-tunity for a long undisturbed discussion. Ahurole unreservedly poured out her domestic troubles and emphasized the role played by Ihuoma.

'I would never have believed it from anybody's lips but yours. I always thought she was a decent woman,' Wonuma said.

'No, mother, she is the quiet dog that eats up the hen's eggs without a bark.'

'Do you think you would settle down with Ekwe if her inter-ference were removed?'

'Nne, I think so.'

Wonuma pondered for some time twitching her right great toe.

'There is an easy way of solving this,' she announced at last.

'How, mother?'

'Anyika will do it.'

Ahurole arched her eyebrows in alarm.

'I don't understand.'

'Don't be alarmed, I am not saying we should poison anyone.'

'Nne, I know you can't say that of course, but . . .'

'I am thinking of something that can draw Ekwe towards you and make him forget Ihuoma.'

'A love potion.'

'Yes.'

'Will it work?'

'There is nothing medicine men cannot achieve. You will go to Anyika as soon as possible – I shall give you the money – you will go to Anyika and ask him to prepare a simple love charm that will bind your husband securely to you. There is nothing wicked in this; many a good wife has done it. It is a matter of protecting your interest – and his, for that matter.'

'Will it be something that will have to be added to his food?'

'Usually there are two sides to it. The first is purely an invocation. The soul of the man concerned is invoked and commanded to love or be destroyed. The second part is a love potion, a simple preparation which is added to the soup.'

'But we normally eat from the same pot. Would it matter if I took in the potion too?'

'It would.'

'Then I can't administer it.'

'Listen, child, you are young and yet to learn many things. You will have to prepare two pots of soup – one for him and one for you.'

'But that would be suspicious, Nne.'

'Hear me out. Women from time to time have to prepare separate pots of soup for themselves in order to include special leaves which keep the womb in good working order. Ekwe's mother prepares it herself, I am sure. All you need to do is to complain of stomach pains. Adaku will prescribe the leaves herself. If she doesn't, suggest it.'

'I think that is all right, mother, but I still wonder whether Ekwe will not be harmed in any way. He is not really a bad man. The trouble is . . . Well I do offend him at times.'

'Do you think I would suggest anything that would harm your husband?'

'No, Nne.'

'Well then meet Anyika tomorrow and get everything settled.'

Ahurole went back to Omokachi with mixed feelings. The idea of a love charm seemed good, but she dreaded having to carry out the processes. They seemed too involved. She wondered whether her attitude while it was being administered would not give her away. But she knew of no other way of dealing with the problem and she was accustomed to taking her mother's advice. After all, from all indications, her mother had subjected her father to the same treatment with apparently good results. Maybe, she thought, marriage was impossible without this type of aid.

The next day when Ekwueme was off to his traps his wife went to see the medicine man. Anyika was out collecting herbs. But his door was open and a fire glowed within. It was typical of Anyika

158

to leave his door open when he was away. Who would dare go in to take anything? Ahurole stood near the door waiting.

'Ah, my daughter, you have been waiting for me.' Ahurole looked back startled. She saw Anyika emerging from the bush, herbs in hand.

'I have not waited long,' she managed to say. Anyika always scared her.

'Come in and sit down,' the medicine man said. Going in was easy but sitting down was not. Most of the chairs had charms and cowries around them. They were all black with age and several had old, dark stains of blood. She hesitated until Anyika pointed to a particular chair.

'I don't blame you, my daughter, for being afraid,' Anyika said, 'some of my chairs are not really meant for humans. Right now there are invisible occupants in them.' A chill ran through the young woman and she wished she had left the whole business to her mother. Anyika noticed her fears and smiled to reassure her.

'Have you brought a message from someone or are you here on your own behalf?'

'On my behalf.'

'On yours? Let me see.' The medicine man reached out for his divination cowries. 'Let's have two manillas,' he said. Ahurole produced them and he set to work. He smiled after a few throws of the cowries and looked up.

'No, my daughter, I don't do it,' he said. Ahurole looked thoroughly worried and simply stared at him.

'I mean I don't administer love potions,' he further explained.

'But I have not told you what I came for,' the young woman said bewildered.

'You don't need to, it is right here on the cowries. Only second-rate medicine men do such stuff. Anyika is above that. I can never raise my hand against anyone in this village. True I am a stranger but I can claim to be a part of the village. What affects it affects me too.'

'But it wouldn't harm him,' Ahurole put in.

'In the long run it might, my daughter. I am sure you have seen active and intelligent men suddenly become passive, stupid and dependent. That is what a love potion can do. So go and settle your differences with your husband peacefully. If you insist, then you must go somewhere else.'

159

Disappointed but impressed Ahurole left Anyika's house. The next day her mother came to visit her. She disclosed her interview with Anyika.

'I shall go to Chiolu myself and arrange this,' Wonuma announced with determination. 'It is very necessary.'

CHAPTER TWENTY-FOUR

A medicine man at Chiolu decanted a brown powder onto his palm. He faced the sun and blew the powder into the air. He re peated the action three times and mumbled certain incantations. He then went back into his room and faced Wonuma.

'I have done it; the man is fixed,' he said, handing Wonuma a packet.

'That is the stuff which your daughter will mix with her husband's food. She need not continue after three market days.'

Wonuma, accompanied by her son, set out on her way back to Omigwe. The problem was solved. Her daughter should settle down now to a stable married life. One thing disturbed her. She had to pass the shrine of Mini Wekwu, the stream that formed the boundary between Chiolu and Omokachi. It was believed that no one carrying any form of poison could cross it unharmed. Many wizards were said to have perished there.

As Wonuma approached the stream-god her fears grew until her legs quaked. She stopped under a tree to rest and debated within herself whether to cross the stream or to go back to Chiolu to get adequate protection from the medicine man. Ah, but what a fool she was. The stuff could not really be classified as poison. If anything it was medicine which was meant to build a home. This conviction grew until she actually felt a sense of pride in having the pluck to seek the welfare of Ahurole and her husband. Mini Wekwu should be proud of her, she thought. She crossed the stream. At Omokachi she handed over the drug to her daughter unobtrusively.

The next day Ahurole complained of serious stomach troubles. Her mother-in-law recommended special leaves to alleviate her pains and by the evening two pots of soup were ready in her kitchen. How easy it had all been. There were no hitches at all. It all seemed so natural. Nevertheless Ahurole's hands trembled as she scooped the recommended dose of the love drug into her husband's soup. The victim did not notice anything as the drug was practically tasteless.

*

A day or two later Ekwueme had slight muscular pains which he attributed to ordinary physical activities. The aches disappeared but then he felt weaker. His mother diagnosed malaria and collected fresh anti-fever leaves. These were boiled up and he used the resulting brown liquid for a bath. It did some good and the fever left him. Then came stomach pains. For days he wriggled in discomfort. According to him he felt as if there were soldier ants in his belly, biting, scratching remorselessly. He was not surprised when he noticed traces of blood in his stool. Clearly he was suffering from dysentery. Anyika gave him some drugs, which worked.

As the dysentery disappeared he was afflicted with rashes and his body itched. He remembered that while trapping he had crossed a farm with a protective ring of charms round it. It was a loose surrounding fence made from climbers, but anyone could tell it was impregnated with ogbara – a charm whose peculiar quality was to cause persistent rashes on the skins of trespassers. Ekwueme knew that the owner of the farm was in fact Mmam, who was notorious for his indiscriminate use of ogbara. He ringed even his pear trees with it and the most intrepid boy would not dream of plucking his pears. It was just like him of course to be strict over everything.

'I am sorry, Ekwe,' Mmam apologized. 'It was meant for heartless folks who push down yams and use the yam-stands as firewood.'

'It was my fault really. I ought to have seen it,' Ekwe said.

'Any new songs?'

'None, Mmam. I have been sickly of late.'

'Don't worry, the rashes will disappear,' the drummer said as he rubbed Ekwe's body with the antidote. In a few days they did.

Joint pains followed. For a trapper nothing could be more incapacitating. Ekwueme found it difficult to bend over his traps. His wrists, ankles and knees were particularly uncomfortable. He knew the answer – a regular steam bath. Twice a day he bent over a pot full of boiling water and roots, covering himself up with a wrapper so that the issuing steam completely enveloped him. Joint pains are usually persistent, returning on and off.

Later Ekwueme developed boils under each armpit and he felt downcast.

162

'Mother,' he complained, 'I never seem to be whole these days. If it is not dysentery it is headache.'

'You are too restless Ekwe,' Adaku said.

'I do nothing outside my normal business. No, I feel there is something definitely wrong with me.' Ahurole had no comments to make on these complaints. It was all she could do to keep up appearances. She had a strong conviction that the medicine man from Chiolu had concocted something not quite as harmless as he had made her mother believe. In her anxiety she forgot about her quarrels with her husband. Ekwueme was now more accommodating though in a dull sort of way. Ahurole herself had cut down her crying. She was more attentive, more withdrawn, less taut. From a sniffing silly girl she had apparently grown into a quiet, stable, mature woman overnight. Wigwe watched the transformation with joy and fascination. The young couple had passed over the difficult phases. It was too good to be true.

When his boils cleared Ekwueme actually expected some more illness, but nothing turned up this time. He went about his traps feeling if not very fresh at least well. His mother said he was putting on weight and jokingly commended Ahurole for her good cooking.

As the days passed by, Adaku was proved right. Ekwueme was putting on weight but he was growing duller. His steps were less springy. He could not wake up at the second cock-crow to make for his traps. He stared at people vacantly and talked less. He startled one or two old men when he passed them by in the morning without offering a greeting. Even when he apologized, his voice sounded strange. His parents observed these transformations with considerable perplexity. Their son was not what he used to be. The spark was gone; but then he was not ill, and they could not suggest that he should go to Anyika. It might annoy him. For a time they had to be content with just watching him. But one day his mother spoke up.

'Ekwe.'

'Yes, mother.'

'Are you well?'

'Of course.'

'Quite sure?'

'Sure. Why do you ask?'

'Nothing in particular. You just look dull these days.'

'Maybe I do, but didn't you say I needed a rest?'

'I did, my son.'

'Well?' Ekwueme said gazing at his mother in an indifferent way that cut her deep. Her eyes smarted and she suppressed the lump in her throat.

'When your father suffered a general weakness last year,' she said, 'Anyika made up a potent drug for him. It is in a small pot and hangs over my hearth. Wouldn't you like to take some of it? All we need do is add a little palm wine.'

'What is all this about?' Ekwueme suddenly flared out. 'I just can't see what you are pestering me for. Please go away, mother.' Adaku slunk away more worried than ever. She was now convinced that all was not well. She called Ahurole in.

'Have you been watching your husband these few days?' She asked searching the younger woman's face.

'I have. Is anything the matter?'

'Anything? Your husband is positively sick. Young women these days are unobservant and most insensitive. If I can detect a change in your husband, I don't see why you can't.'

'But, mother, there is nothing wrong with him,' Ahurole said as blandly as she could.

'My child your husband is ill, very ill. What of, I can't say but he is ill, very ill. Even his manner of speaking has changed. Think of the man you married last year. Think of the empty thing before you now. Ahurole, you must be blind. No, it can't be. You are pretending not to notice because you are the cause.'

Ahurole's knees wobbled with fear. She had been found out. But Adaku's next words, though furious, reassured the young woman.

'Yes, it is you and your nagging. You have turned him inside-out. You are . . .'

'What is it, Adaku?' Wigwe said stooping at the doorway and holding on to the bamboo framework of the low roof. Adaku could not explain. She suddenly realized that strong though her feelings were she had no grounds for berating her daughter-in-law the way she was doing. Wigwe turned to Ahurole.

'What is it?'

'She called me in and asked me what was wrong with Ekwueme. I told her I did not feel anything was particularly wrong with him and she began to scold me.'

164

'Go back to your house, Ahurole. Adaku, you will tell me all about it later.'

In the evening of that day Wigwe called Adaku into his inner room and closed the door.

'What was it?' He asked staring at his wife intently.

'What do you think of our son?' was the answering question.

'He looks bad.'

'I say he looks very bad. He is half the man he was, my lord.'

'What do you think is wrong with him?'

'I suspect he has been bewitched, my lord.'

'So do I, but by whom?'

'The world is a bad place, my lord. It is often difficult to say who are friends and who enemies.'

'Shall we go to Anyika?'

'What else?'

'On Nkwo?'

'Let me see, today is Eke, tomorrow Irie, the next Awho, then Nkwo. Four days. Too long.'

'Awho then.'

'All right.'

'Meanwhile we shall watch him closely.'

•

For the second day Ekwueme had not inspected his traps. He had been strolling about the compound hardly speaking to anyone. He avoided people, particularly his wife. He ate little. He was now emaciated and the shadows round his eyes lent him a lost look. His father interviewed him in his room.

'What about your traps, Ekwe?' he asked.

'Doing fine.'

'It doesn't look as if you have inspected them for some time.' Ekwueme laughed outright. His father was terribly shocked.

'What are you laughing at?' he asked timidly. His son looked at him and laughed still more.

'Ekwueme!' Laughter greeted his call.

'Ekwueme!!' His son only laughed more loudly.

Wigwe turned round and sought for his wife. She had gone to the farm. He was nearly frantic. He went back to take another look at his son. He was still in his room, lying on his bed quietly. A contented smile, the remnant of the laughter that had frightened

165

his father, still played on his face. He was facing the wall and gesticulating with his fingers, oblivious of his father's presence. He was mumbling to himself but much like someone having an interesting *tête-à-tête* with someone else. Wigwe stood rooted at the door. He moistened his lips several times to speak. Each time he failed and swallowed hard instead. He coughed to attract his son's attention. Ekwueme turned round and gazed past his father for all the world as if he were not standing there. Sickened, Wigwe went back to his room, extracted two manillas from a hole under his bed and made for Anyika's. The medicine man was not at home. Wigwe came back and sat on a chair in his reception hall in a position where he could have a full view of the door of his son's room. From his point of vantage he could see Ekwueme's legs. They played about restlessly, the toes twitching. As it was, Wigwe could do nothing for the moment other than keep a strict watch on the young man.

As soon as his wife came back, Wigwe half staggered into her house.

'Adaku, our son has been terribly bewitched. He ... He is not himself. I wonder whether he even recognizes me.'

'Chei! Has it come to that?' With that Adaku tried to rush out. Her husband held her fast.

'Listen,' he said, 'we must show as little excitement as possible; firstly for his sake, secondly to keep the affair secret. We shall continue to talk to him as if we suspect nothing until Anyika comes back.'

'I understand, my lord, but I must see him first,' the distraught woman said.

'Before you see him, call his wife and let me give her the same advice.'

'She is not back yet from the farm,' Adaku said and went off to see her son. Half-way her eyes filled with tears. She went back and wiped her eyes carefully and assumed as nonchalant an air as she could.

'Ekwe, are you sleeping?' she asked.

'No,' he said.

'You have been indoors today.'

Ekwueme declined to reply. His mother studied him intently, then went and sat by him. She touched him all over with her open palm. Ekwueme lay quiescent. Encouraged Adaku spoke again.

166

'Do you feel any pains inside you?'

'There you go again,' Ekwueme said, half rising from his bed.

'Can't I be left alone for a time? I can't understand this at all. Everybody seems off his or her mind. All right, you take over the house.' With that he rose quickly and disappeared through the doorway.

CHAPTER TWENTY-FIVE

Adaku ran after her son, but the sickening dread in her mind deadened her legs. She could not overtake him and she shouted in desperation. Alarmed, Wigwe came out of the reception hall in time to see his son running out of the compound. He planted himself in his path and stretched out his arms sideways to intercept him. Ekwueme collected him and flung him into a humiliating heap. Wigwe was far more alarmed than hurt. He scrambled up and gave chase to his son who was rapidly increasing the distance between them.

Wigwe knew it was hopeless trying to chase him alone. He stopped running and took a deep breath to shout but changed his mind. Instead he headed straight for Mmam's house. Mmam was drying some drums in the sun having rubbed the skins over with palm oil. He glanced at Wigwe and let go the drum he had in hand. He had never seen the old man so agitated.

'Is all well?' he inquired anxiously. For answer Wigwe signalled him into the nearest room.

'Are you busy?' he asked hoarsely.

'Not particularly,' Mmam replied trying to peer into the face of the white-haired man.

'Ekwe is ... Ekwe is ... Ekwe has run away. Come and help me find him.'

'Run away? What for? Where to?'

'No time for questions, Mmam. Let's get others to help.'

Mmam sprang outside half dragging the old man with him. His wife stared after him as he moved away rapidly with Wigwe. She did not bother him with questions. She was content to wait and learn afterwards. Over the years she had discovered that Mmam was a man of few words and that he had fewer words still to offer when actively engaged. The two men collected two other men – Nnadi and Wakiri – and together they set out without saying anything to anyone.

*

It had been a busy day for Ahurole at the farm. She hardly noticed that the sun was journeying to Chiolu as she weeded energetically. She wanted to make up for the time she lost in the earlier part of the day thinking about her domestic problems. Then she had found it difficult to settle down to work. Her mind had been filled with a vague but powerful dread for the future. Her husband's recent behaviour made her feel guilty and miserable. When her husband showed the first signs of unusual discomforts she had promptly stopped administering the love drug, but this did not make her feel any less guilty.

The crying of a cuckoo in the neighbouring bush made her straighten up. She looked at her shadow. It had grown quite long. Twilight was not far ahead. Quickly she gathered some firewood, and collected two types of vegetables. She was too tired to carry anything heavy, besides no one was near enough to help her. So she made her basket as light as possible and walked home-wards.

She half expected either to overtake or to be overtaken by some neighbours who would provide company for the journey home. Today she passed the farms without anyone joining her. She did not mind. Her thoughts provided company, perhaps too much company. Also the forests were no longer 'unhealthy'. The dead chief had long been buried. She walked on, her squeaking basket beating out the pace. She passed the shrine of Ali the earth-god, and later the shrine of Amadioha. Now she could hear the distant chatter of the colony of weaver birds nesting on several palm trees in the middle of the village.

She rounded a bend and a long section of the path stretched out before her. A man emerged from the bend far ahead of her, lum-bering along much like a child sent on an errand he wouldn't have undertaken but for the promise of a piece of meat. A little later she recognized the man as her husband; at the same moment, Ekwueme looked up and saw his wife. He increased his speed.

This change of pace alarmed Ahurole and she stood still, her heart beating wildly. Ekwueme could not be going to inspect his traps so late in the day. He had no matchet anyway. Somehow this reassured her. He only had a walking-stick which seemed to bother him as he ran. Still he clutched it tightly.

What worried Ahurole was the fact that he looked intently at her as he ran. He was not paying much attention to the path and occasionally went off course and trampled on the wayside weeds. His looks were wild and far from affectionate. He was gathering speed too. Unconsciously Ahurole took one step back and then another. Ekwueme saw this and sprang forward at full trot. His sudden acceleration jerked the stick out of his hand. He stopped, turned back, picked it up and raced towards his wife, his wrapper trailing behind him. Now Ahurole was convinced he was making for her but her legs simply refused to move. A few paces from her, Ekwueme brandished his stick. Ahurole saw his mouth foaming. Desperately she flung her basket down and slipped into the bush. Ekwueme stumbled over the basket and crashed heavily. He did not seem to mind. He got up quickly and inspected the basket. Among other things it contained a small earthen jug with a little water in it. Miraculously it had not been broken. He took it up, threw his head backwards and drank like a thirsty frog.

Ahurole out of a compelling curiosity stopped at a distance and watched her husband. When he had drunk he dashed the pot to pieces and kicked the basket which disgorged its contents along the path. He breathed heavily. He seemed to have forgotten all about her. Ahurole wondered what to do. One plan would be to creep far into the bush and emerge into the path a long way off and race homewards. But then she was bound to attract his attention while moving through the bush. Ekwueme was much used to the bush and would capture her with ease if he wanted to. No, the best thing was to hit the path at the nearest point from where she was and run for it. The village was not far off and with luck she might make it. But she could not summon enough energy to move. She began to toy with the idea of hiding where she was until someone came along. But it was near twilight and she knew that most people had gone home.

She looked at her husband again. He just sat there as if he was in his reception hall. He seemed to have no purpose. She was completely baffled. Then her nerves began to give way. Her balance faltered and she broke a twig. At the noise Ekwueme looked up and his face lit up. As he made to rise, Ahurole sprang into the path and fled. Ekwueme ran in pursuit. For a time Ahurole gained on him. She could tell from the dying sound of his steps. Then she looked back, stumbled and fell. Ekwueme increased his pace and by the time she scrambled up he was very close. She started running again but with less energy; the fall had weakened her con-

170

siderably and she was bruised in several places. As Ekwueme gained on her she started to scream.

She rounded a bend and faced four men at full trot. Mmam was in the lead.

'Where is he?' Wigwe gasped. Immediately afterwards Ekwueme bore down on them. Mmam grabbed him by the waist and they rolled together into the bush. The other men came and they overpowered him. He lay on the ground panting, mouth foaming, eyes closed. Wigwe looked at the young men and the young men looked at him. Wigwe's face seemed more wrinkled, his hair whiter. He shook his head slowly from side to side and ground his strong teeth. Ekwueme opened his eyes. They had a vacant care-free look that scared the men surrounding him.

'Ekwe,' Wakiri called him.

'Wakiri the wag,' he replied lightly, 'what are you holding me for? Have you turned crazy too? Let me go.' The men realized talking would not do. It was best to be silent.

Twilight was deepening rapidly now and they had barely enough light to see the path by. They dragged Ekwueme along with them as gently as was possible. At first he was difficult but later he followed them obediently. Just before they got to the edge of the village, Wigwe told them to halt.

'Let's wait for the darkness,' he said. 'People must not see my son in this condition. It is unbearable. I shall go to the house to prepare his wife and his mother to receive him. Wait here until I come.'

The old man left them, his head bowed. Left alone with Ekwe the young men were too embarrassed to talk. The whole episode looked like a nightmare and they rubbed their eyes in vain to wake from the evil dream. They could not look at him. They just held him and turned away their faces. Wakiri was perhaps the most affected. For once he could not talk, much less joke. His large eyes were red with suppressed weeping.

Wigwe came back and they shepherded Ekwueme into his room. They could not bring themselves to lock him in, so Nnadi and Wakiri kept watch while Mmam went off to inform his wife that he would be away for the rest of the evening. Clearly, there was only one thing to be done – call in Anyika.

'Stay with him,' Wigwe said to the men, 'while I fetch Anyika.' As he turned to go, someone brushed by him swiftly and violently.

171

He looked back and saw Nnadi and Wakiri darting out of the room. He understood at once: Ekwueme had escaped.

It was a dark night. Tracking a man in the forest was the job of the village. Wigwe knew he would come in for much blame if he tried to carry on alone or with just a few men. He contacted the village head and in the still evening air, the Ikoro or talking drum rang out. The last time it was heard was when Madume was found hanging in his room. The women quaked in their kitchens while every male who was of age dashed to the arena with his matchet and club.

'Wigwe,' Nwokekoro said, 'we shall leave the search to the younger men. By morning your son should be safe with you. Amadioha will see to that. Meanwhile go to Anyika for divination.' And in the time it took a man to gulp down a meal, the forest surrounding Omokachi was alive with men on the alert.

The older men went home, Anyika among them. Like every other man he had to obey the call of the Ikoro. He walked home now, a faint smile on his face. He had seen it happen before. He was particularly touched by this because he rather liked Ekwueme. He thought of Wigwe and quickened his pace. He knew he would come looking for him very soon. As for the divination he hardly needed his famous cowries. It was plain enough; the symptoms were unmistakable. What was more, Ahurole had come to him for a love potion.

As he hurried home a figure passed by him rapidly in the darkness. He thought it was a woman since it appeared to be dressed in a full wrapper. It was youthful judging from the pace. No woman would be about at such an hour unless she was running away. He wondered who had quarrelled with her husband. His mind ran through many young married women. What a fool he was; Ahurole of course. He got home to find Wigwe and Adaku waiting for him, manillas in hand. Quickly he set to work.

He had reckoned he wouldn't need his famous cowries but there was no telling what side issues were involved. So he brought them out and after a few throws, was pouring out the whole story to the astonished parents. When he had done he said:

'You will probably not find Ahurole at home when you get back.'

'Perhaps not. If she has really done this she dare not face us.'

'Did you say "if"?' Anyika asked with a mirthless smile.

172

'Anyika, don't be annoyed. I am not doubting your divination,' Wigwe apologized.

'As for his cure,' Anyika went on, 'I shall give him an antidote. The only difficulty is getting him to take the medicine of his own free will. I shall ask him if he wants to be cured. If the answer is yes, all will be well; if not, things will be difficult indeed.'

'Can't you make him say yes?' Adaku asked.

'Of course I can but I shall not.'

'Why?'

'The antidote would still not work.'

'Let's wait until we find him,' Wigwe said and rose to go.

There was no talk of the evening meal; Wigwe and his wife sat in their reception hall shivering with nervous fever. Nkechi made a fire for them and shared their vigil. She was too frightened to go to bed alone. When she grew sleepy she spread a mat by her parents and slept at their feet.

Some elderly men and women gathered to give sympathy and to sit up with them through the long lonely night. The women sat around Adaku and supported her, doing their best to calm her. Occasionally someone would scold her sternly when she threatened to lose control. Ekwueme would be all right, they said. They cited several cases and argued that if anything Ekwueme's case was a mild one.

The men talked in low voices amongst themselves. They did not try to console Wigwe directly. But they channelled their conversation along encouraging lines.

'I won't be surprised if the men find him quite soon,' Chima said.

'Quite possible,' Nwokekoro confirmed. 'He can't go far in this darkness.'

'You remember the day Olulu got lost in the Great Ponds?' Chima asked.

'Who can forget it?' Webilo replied.

'He was not lost in the Great Ponds though,' Wosu said.

'You are right,' Webilo said. 'It was in the Nkata forest near the Great Ponds. I have forgotten what he went to do there.'

'To collect some canes for making baskets for his wife,' Wosu said. 'I remember that because I was among those who found him sleeping under a tree. The canes – magnificent canes they were – the canes lay in a neat bundle by him. When we woke him he called on his wife to put away the canes.'

173

'Was his wife there?' Chima asked.

'Of course not,' Wosu went on, 'the man had been dreaming. It took him some time to realize where he was. Then he thanked us profusely and walked home with us.'

'I hope he won't get lost again tonight,' Chima said. A few people laughed half-heartedly. It was hardly the time for a joke.

'Are there any young men who know the positions of Ekwe's traps?' Webilo asked. 'He is more likely to use the tracks leading to his traps.'

'That is a point,' Wosu said, 'I wish we had thought about it before the boys set out.'

'They would probably reason the same way,' Nwokekoro said.

The night wore on. One by one the women felt drowsy and retired. Two or three men went with them. The rest stayed on telling tales of lost men and of survival in the forest.

As people stirred from their first sleep, the moon rose. Men's hopes rose with it.

'They should find him now,' Webilo said.

'The forests are dark even by moonlight,' Chima pointed out. 'A man would look the same as the trees.'

'Still, a moving man can be detected.'

A cock crew at Omigwe. Others replied from Omokachi. The night was half gone.

'Wigwe, I think you should go to sleep now,' Nwokekoro said, 'I am sure your son will be by you in the morning. A good night's sleep should help you face your difficulties. Remember you will have much to do in the next few days.'

Wigwe looked up, shook his head, and sat back against his chair, his chin resting on his chest. Several men joined Nwokekoro and persuaded him to go to bed.

For a long time, Wigwe lay awake with his thoughts. Ekwe was mad, was that it? It couldn't be true; it just could not be. Ekwe his only son, mad. He had two sons but the other was a baby. He was as good as a man with just one son, he thought. One son and that one dead. Dead, yes. A mad son was as good as a dead one, probably worse. His wife interrupted his thoughts.

'My lord.'

'Yes, Adaku.'

'Do you think Ekwe is mad?'

174

'No.'

'Why is he behaving this way?'

'It is the love potion.'

'Will he get better?'

'He will.'

'Do you think he will take Anyika's drug willingly?'

'He will.' If she broke into tears who would stop her at such a time of the night?

'Do you remember anyone suffering from this type of thing, my lord?'

'Yes.'

'Who?'

'Not in this village.'

'Where?'

'Aliji.'

'Did he get better?'

'I think he did. I did not stay at Aliji long enough to see his complete recovery, but he was making some progress while I was there.'

'When was this?'

'I was quite a young man then. I had gone to Aliji for a big wrestling contest.'

'My lord, I am afraid.'

'Ekwe will be all right. Amadioha cannot forsake us at this hour. We have never missed a sacrifice.'

'To think of him alone in the forest all through the night is unbearable,' Adaku said sniffing.

'Hush, remember he is a trapper. He is used to the forest. He knows which parts are dangerous and which are not.'

'But he is not quite himself.'

'He is not mad. He is only disturbed. I am sure he will look after himself as well as he can.'

'Oh! Amadioha, please help our son! You gave him to us, don't forsake him now.' Adaku's prayer threatened to end in a sob but Wigwe said encouragingly:

'He may not even be in the bush.'

'What do you mean?' Adaku said with some excitement.

'He could be hiding right in the village, in one corner of some-one's reception hall.'

'That is possible,' Adaku said brightening up. 'He may come

175

back. Let me look in his room.' Before her husband could stop her she undid the door and ran off to her son's house. Wigwe waited for a time. When his wife did not appear he went out to look for her. He found her in his son's empty room, weeping bitterly.

The cock crew again.

CHAPTER TWENTY-SIX

The morning came and with it dull-eyed young men who had walked the forest all night in search of their comrade. They had not been able to trace him. They came back for a bath and breakfast after which they would resume their search.

When the Ikoro sounded once more the arena was packed full with anxious men and women. The men were mostly quiet, trying to brace themselves for the job ahead. The women did most of the talking. Some were chatting animately, others weeping, still others were just sad-eyed. They discussed Ekwueme's wife and her flight. It was horrible, they all agreed; she was a disgrace to her village.

Ihuoma was one of the women who came to see the men off. Nnenda was by her side and they conversed in low tones. She was not among the weeping but those two lines appeared on her brow. She seemed to be feeling chilly too since she had an extra wrapper around her shoulders.

The men massed themselves under a shady tree to discuss their line of action. Nwokekoro was the first to speak out.

'Who knows Ekwe's traps?' he asked.

'I do,' Nnadi replied raising his right hand unconsciously.

'You will go with a group of men and search the tracks leading to as many of his traps as you know. Others will go anywhere else they believe holds out some hope.' Five other men grouped themselves around Nnadi. Mmam was among them. He said:

'Nnadi, we need one thing for this journey.'

'What?'

'Dogs.'

'Yes, we will take them along. We had some last night.'

'I mean Ekwe's dogs.'

'He has none.'

'Any from his father's compound will do.'

'See if you can fetch one quickly.'

Soon the surrounding bushes swallowed the men. Nnadi led his team to the entrance of one of the tracks leading to Ekwueme's traps. There Mmam joined them, leading a white-and-brown dog.

177

After a few paces they fanned out, Mmam occupying the track itself. The dog moved ahead, sometimes along the track, sometimes out of it, dodging in and out of the undergrowths.

By the time the sun was overhead they had inspected several traps belonging to the lost man. Two traps had animals in them. One was so rotten they had to leave it alone. Nnadi carried the other.

'I know no other traps,' Nnadi announced at last. 'We shall have to work along the open forest now.'

'I know just one,' Wakiri said.

'Where?'

'Very close to the village, in fact from there you can hear people talking in his father's compound.'

'He can't be there,' Mmam said decisively. 'Wakiri, this is not a plan to send us home, is it?'

'Mmam, I am not joking,' Wakiri said simply.

'I think he is serious,' Nnadi said studying Wakiri's face.

'He is a joker, but since this search began I have not seen him laugh.'

'I love to see him serious for once,' Mmam teased.

'I wouldn't be if you were lost though,' Wakiri said.

'You don't need to tell me,' Mmam retorted smiling.

'The trouble is useless fellows like you never get lost.'

'There he goes, didn't I say he could never do without a joke?'

'I have always associated you with drumming. I didn't know you could talk quite so much.' The laugh was on Mmam and he fell silent.

When Nnadi's group arrived at the village they made straight for Wigwe's compound and deposited the animal from Ekwueme's trap. They decided to have a look at the trap trail behind Wigwe's compound before coming back for a rest. As soon as they set out, the white-and-brown dog shot forwards. The men broke into a run when they heard it barking ahead. When they got there they saw nothing. But the dog kept barking and refused to move. The men formed a circle round it and spread out. Still they drew blank. Wakiri came back and observed that the dog was barking up a tree. He looked up and saw Ekwueme resting on a comfortable branch of the tree. A slight shudder ran through him. He could not shout. His throat was dry. For a time he gazed at his friend, who was unaware of his presence. It was indeed Ekwueme. He was dangling his legs absent-mindedly and biting his left thumb. His right arm was hooked around a branch for stability.

Wakiri moved quietly over to Nnadi and told him of his discovery. They decided it would be best not to raise any alarm. Quietly they informed the other men. Then they all moved away from the tree and had a short discussion. In the end they decided to leave the three men behind to keep watch while the rest went back to the village. Wakiri volunteered to stay behind. He retired with the other two to a hidden but clear point of vantage and waited.

Nnadi and the rest moved as casually as their excitement would let them into the village. They passed Wigwe's compound without informing him of their find. They guessed he would get very excited and scare his son away. Instead they went to Nwokekoro. The Ikoro was sounded and as its sound sped from tree to tree, the surrounding forest gradually disgorged the men it had swallowed. Wigwe and red-eyed Adaku came hurrying down with Nkechi trotting behind them. They searched the arena for Ekwueme. Their sorrow deepened. He would die after three days if he was not found, Wigwe thought.

As soon as Nwokekoro saw Ekwueme's distressed parents he drew them aside and had a short talk with them. Their faces lit up and Adaku raised her hands in thanksgiving to Amadioha.

'Ekwueme has been found,' Nwokekoro announced. 'He is somewhere near the village with some men. I thank you all for your great show of devotion. You will not be able to see him right away. As you know, he is hungry and tired and needs a lot of rest; but in a day or two you should be able to see him. I guess that within eight days, he will be singing in this arena.'

A great sigh swept through the crowd when Nwokekoro mentioned singing. Wigwe thanked the young men and went off with Nwokekoro by his side.

Wigwe ordered Nkechi to make a hot bath ready for his son. As for food, that had always been in readiness ever since Ekwueme disappeared. Nnadi and Mmam led the way to where Ekwueme was. Wigwe looked up at his son and was speechless for a long time. But Adaku was beside herself.

'Come down, my son,' she cried hoarsely, 'come down. Oh thanks be to Amadioha. Ojukwu, I thank you too. Ekwe, you have nearly killed us. Oh come down, let me touch you, come down.'

During this outburst everyone was quiet. All eyes were fixed on the haggard figure on the tree. Ekwueme did not move. Once or twice he looked down at the people and continued to chew his

179

thumb. He did nothing else to show his awareness of the people below. Nnadi spoke to him in the most persuasive tone. Wakiri and Mmam did the same but it was all lost on the fugitive. Gradually the initial joy of discovery was replaced by a fearful doubt of Ekwueme's sanity. True, this possibility had been in many people's minds but with Ekwueme sitting up the tree and paying no attention to anyone the probability assumed a dreadful certainty, Wigwe spoke:

'Mmam, go up the tree and persuade him to come down.' Mmam adjusted the flying tails of his wrapper and began to climb slowly up the tree. When he got to the first branch he paused and looked Ekwueme over. Carefully he continued his ascent. His quarry looked at him in a dull sort of way and for the first time stopped chewing his thumb. He stretched out his left hand and from a confused network of climbers and branches near him drew out a hitherto unseen club.

'Look out!' someone shouted from below. Mmam descended rapidly to the lowest branch, panting.

The realization that matters were far more complicated than they thought jolted everyone. Slowly the space around the tree filled up with people from the village. Eventually even women began to turn up. They approached cautiously either holding on to the arms of men or clutching the nearest sapling.

Suddenly Adaku raised a loud wail. She flung herself on the ground and rolled over several times before strong arms held her. Then everyone started talking at once. They pleaded, they threatened, they abused Ekwueme. Nothing was achieved. He sat up there club in hand and apparently looking at the top of a palm tree close at hand. His air of unconcern made the onlookers feel helpless. If only he had no club, some said. As people got tired of standing around, helplessness gave way to desperation. The young men grouped themselves together and held a spirited discussion. Three men volunteered to go up and dare his attack. As they were getting ready to go, someone pointed out that even if they disarmed him, bringing him down without his consent would be a problem. For one thing, only one man could get to him at a time; for another violence was out of the question as he might fall off his high perch. The volunteers stood around the tree caressing it, and looking around for other suggestions. Then Nwokekoro spoke out in his loud, clear voice.

'Ekwe, I order you to come down. You know what powers I carry with me. You know whom I represent. He is right here now and he has commanded me to order you down.'

Ekwueme mumbled something. People surged forward and cupped their ears with their hands to catch the sound. It was throaty and incoherent but it was greatly encouraging.

'What did you say?' Nwokekoro shouted up the tree. Again Ekwueme mumbled something which no one could understand.

'Mmam, go up the tree again and see if you can catch what he is saying,' Wigwe said. Mmam clambered up again and, keeping a close watch on him, went as far as he dared.

'Now tell Mmam what it is you want,' Nwokekoro shouted again, his white beard vibrating. Mmam relayed the message and Ekwueme's lips moved again.

'I am hearing something like Ihuoma,' Mmam said to the people below. A murmur ran through the crowd and people's glances darted hither and thither looking for Ihuoma. She was not there.

'What about Ihuoma?' Nwokekoro asked. Again the patient crowd had to wait while Mmam and Ekwueme exchanged a most curious conversation.

'He says he wants Ihuoma,' Mmam relayed. Another murmur rose from the crowd. A lunatic always has his whims and Nwokekoro decided to exploit them.

'If Ihuoma comes will you come down?'

Ekwueme nodded slowly. Ihuoma was sent for. People made way for her as she came up. Everyone looked at her curiously but no particular importance was attached to Ekwueme's preference for her. That was the way of lunatics, they always had people they liked and people they disliked so much that they would chase them around any time they set eyes on them. For instance Otudo the madman at the waterside market had a morbid hatred for Nwokekoro. He once threw a cocoyam at him and hit him on the forehead. Still, Ihuoma felt some embarrassment but she knew the worst she could do was to show it.

'Ihuoma is here now, come down Ekwe.'

To everyone's relief the young man began to descend. Fortunately he left the club behind. He was a long time coming down and during that time nothing was heard but the cluck, cluck, cluck of a hen feeding her brood of chickens hard by.

CHAPTER TWENTY-SEVEN

Ekwueme cleared the food set before him. His mother refilled his place and the second helping also disappeared. Adaku was pleased. This was an encouraging sign. When it came to bathing, however, Ekwueme proved difficult. He kicked and broke the earthenware pot. Adaku reluctantly gave up the idea and wondered what she could do to remove the grime on her son's body. His wrapper was in an even worse state. It was torn in several places and much stained.

When Adaku complained about this to her husband, he waved her aside impatiently and went off to call Anyika. Before that he had detailed some young men to remain in the compound and keep an eye on his son.

Anyika came round with his medicine bag. He went into Ekwueme's room followed by Wigwe and his wife. Ekwueme was lying on his bamboo bed. When he saw them he turned his face to the wall.

'Go away you wicked old man,' he said to Anyika. 'Do not worry me. You are mad; all your life you have been mad.'

'You are right Ekwe,' Anyika said, 'turn round and let's talk.'

'I don't want to talk to you, go away.'

'Ekwe . . .'

'Wait, Anyika. Don't put the question to him until he calms down,' Wigwe said.

'I know better than that, my friend Wigwe. I merely want him to get used to my presence, so that he may develop a more friendly attitude.'

'If you think I shall be friends with you, you are mistaken,' Ekwueme cut in.

'We are friends, Ekwe.'

'We are not.'

'We are.'

Anyika stretched out his hand and touched him lightly. He started and jumped out of the bed. Wigwe quickly barred the doorway while Anyika stood on the alert ready to grab him if he tried to run off. He looked over the two men carefully and sat down.

'Wigwe,' he said. 'I have something important to say.' Ekwueme had never called his father by name. Now that he did so Wigwe winced but quickly controlled himself.

'What is it?' he asked with some resignation.

'I want to marry Ihuoma.'

'Oh, that is easy,' his father said.

'I want to marry her now.'

'Yes, but first let us discuss something else.'

'I say I want to marry her now, now, now. Don't you understand?'

'You will marry Ihuoma as soon as we finish our discussion but not until then,' Wigwe insisted desperately.

'Then let us discuss whatever you want. Do you promise I shall marry her today?'

'Oh, right away, my son.'

Wigwe winked at Anyika to proceed. The medicine man tried to fix Ekwueme with his eye and get him to stare back at him, but he couldn't.

'Ekwe, face me,' he said.

Ekwueme faced him with full eyes drained of most of their intelligence.

'You will take this medicine now,' Anyika said slowly and distinctly.

'Is this the discussion you were talking about? Drink your medicine, you crazy fellow, I won't. Get me Ihuoma, I say. I want to marry her. If I don't I shall not listen to anybody, not even Nwokekoro. Medicine? I need no medicine. I am not sick. Ihuoma, Ihuoma, get me Ihuoma.' As he said the last sentence he pulled at his right ear for emphasis. Anyika rose.

'Adaku, come out for a moment,' he said. Outside, Anyika went on:

'If we are to achieve anything at all, Ihuoma must be near by. You see when a mad fellow gets hold of an idea it is impossible to shake him out of it. If you can get Ihuoma and arrange a make-believe marriage, he might take my medicines.'

'Ah, we have disturbed that woman enough. How can we ever bring her to agree to such a clumsy business? Chei, this is getting beyond us. Anyika, will he *ever* recover?'

'I think he will if only he takes the antidote. Discuss my suggestion with your husband and do what you can about it. It seems the only way out.'

'Call him out and discuss it with him yourself,' Adaku said.

'I don't want him to leave the room. Ekwe may escape.'

'You can stay close to the door and speak in whispers. Besides we have some men around in case of emergency.'

Wigwe came out and Anyika put forward his suggestions.

'It is the only thing I can think of. If you succeed in persuading Ihuoma let me know by tomorrow morning.'

With that the medicine man shouldered his sack and went away.

While Mmam and Wakiri kept Ekwueme company Wigwe and his wife interviewed Ihuoma at her house that evening.

'My daughter,' Wigwe began, 'we thank you for the great help you rendered us this afternoon. Many a woman would have hesitated over a situation like that, but you acted promptly and calmly as if you were his sister. Thank you, my daughter. The gods will reward you.'

'There is nothing to thank me for. It was a simple act which anyone might have performed. You don't know how sorry I feel about the whole thing. I wish I could help you even more.'

This was very encouraging and Wigwe followed it up quickly.

'That is just what we have come for,' he said.

'Has he run away again?' Ihuoma asked.

'No. You see he wouldn't take the medicine which Anyika brought along. He kept raving for you. Anyika reckoned that he might drink the medicine if you were around.'

'That is easy. I shall come,' Ihuoma said readily.

'There is another point,' Wigwe went on. 'It may be necessary to make him believe he will marry you later on. You see that also is one of his obsessions.'

Ihuoma thought for awhile. Wigwe watched her anxiously.

'Dede,' she said at last, 'I shall come, but first I shall mention it to Nnadi my brother-in-law. I am sure he won't object but it is only proper he should know my movements.'

'How can I thank you, Ihuoma, my daughter? If ever my son gets well I shall think you played the greatest part towards his recovery.'

Wigwe left feeling full of relief. His wife said to him:

'My lord, I think Ihuoma is the best woman I have ever seen.'

'I have always said so.'

Meanwhile Ihuoma went over to Nnadi's to discuss the new development.

'Of course you may go if that will help. Ekwueme is one of the best young men in the village and we can't afford to lose him.' So Nnadi reassured her and she waited for the morning with a mind too full for words.

The next day after breakfast Nkechi came to fetch her. She took her children to Nnadi's wife and moved over to Wigwe's compound. She was let into Ekwueme's room, where Anyika was already trying unsuccessfully to converse with Ekwueme. As soon as Ihuoma entered Ekwueme's eyes lit up, the dullness left his face, and he relaxed.

'Ekwe.'

'Ihuoma.'

'How are you?'

'I am quite well. It is only these crazy fellows who have been bothering me. Come and sit by me.' The young woman hesitated. Adaku looked at her pleadingly. Ekwueme had not had a bath for days and was stinking but, with a courage and naturalness that disarmed Wigwe and his wife, Ihuoma smiled at Ekwueme and took her seat beside him. He promptly put his arms around her.

'I have not seen you for a long long time, Ihuoma,' he said.

'That is because you ran away from us,' Ihuoma replied. She was treading on delicate ground and Wigwe held his breath. But his son didn't seem to mind.

'People were bothering me.'

'Maybe, but that was no reason for running away.'

'I shall not do it again,' Ekwueme said.

'Please don't.'

Wigwe and the others in the room were almost shocked at Ekwueme's instantaneous change for good. Ihuoma seemed to have absolute power over him.

'Do you know I shall marry you?' Ekwueme asked suddenly.

'Of course I do, but you must first take whatever medicine Anyika may give you,' Ihuoma said.

'I will.'

This seemed a good point at which to break in and the veteran medicine man seized it.

185

'Ekwe, will you take this medicine?' he asked holding up a black lump. Ekwueme looked up and for a moment was undecided. Ihuoma looked at him and he promptly nodded. Wigwe and Adaku were happy. Anyika broke off a piece of the black stuff and dropped it into a coconut shell with some water in it. He made it into a thick paste, added some more water and handed it over to the sick man. Ekwueme drank it down and returned the cup.

'I shall be back in the evening,' Anyika announced as he went off.

'Now, Ekwe, you must bathe. You haven't had a bath for some time now,' Ihuoma said.

'I shall.'

'I mean now.'

'I agree.'

A hot bath was quickly prepared. Wigwe offered to help his son bathe, but the young man waved him off. He made a good job of it nevertheless and rubbed his body over with fresh palm kernel oil. He asked for his comb and it was brought to him. His mother gave him a clean wrapper and he discarded the battered thing he had around him.

Ihuoma stood outside while he changed his clothes. Adaku came round and hugged her affectionately with tears in her eyes.

'See if you can convince him to sleep, my daughter,' Adaku said brightly.

'I shall try,' Ihuoma said and went back into Ekwueme's room. His face broke into a smile as she came in.

'Ekwe, you must be sleepy now.'

'No, I don't want to sleep,' he said emphatically.

Ihuoma realized she had to be more tactful. 'I thought you were tired,' she said.

'I am not tired.'

'What do you want to do now?'

'Chat with you.'

'All right, let's chat.'

Ihuoma remembered she had to feed her children but if she was not to undo the good work she had done she had no choice but to stay and talk.

'Ihuoma, I want to marry you.'

'Ekwe, I thought we had agreed on that.'

'But when?'

'As soon as you take all the medicine Anyika may give you.'

'I shall take it quickly.'

'That would be nice.'

'You know I spent a bad night in the forest.'

Ihuoma thought this was a dangerous trend in their conversation but on second thoughts she let him talk.

'It must have been,' she replied.

'I felt hungry and tired.'

'I am sorry.'

'And I thought about you.'

'Well, if you had not come back you wouldn't have seen me. Look, you must not run away again, Ekwe, or I shall not come here any more.'

'No, I shall not.'

'Tell me, Ekwe, do you feel any pain inside you?'

'No.'

'Sure?'

'Yes.'

'Then you should soon get better.'

'I am well already.'

'Ekwe I want to go and feed my children. Can you sleep while I am away?'

'Will you come back?'

'I shall.'

'Can't I go with you?'

'No.'

'Why?'

'Because Anyika says you must stay here until you have taken all your medicine.'

'Suppose I refuse?'

'Then you won't see me again.'

'All right, I shall stay.'

'That is good.'

As Ihuoma passed by Wigwe's reception hall on her way out, the old man beckoned to her.

'Is he asleep now?' he asked.

'He is about to sleep.'

'Do you think he will run off again?'

'Very unlikely.'

'My child, I can't tell you how grateful we are to you.'

187

'Dede, you are making too much of this.'

'And this after my rudeness to you,' Wigwe pressed on full of remorse.

'You have never done me any wrong, Dede.'

Wigwe regarded the young woman for a while. She was breaking off little bits of dried palm leaves from the low roof of the reception hall and her face was averted.

'Will you come in the evening?'

'As often as you want me to.'

'Thank you, Ihuoma.'

'It is nothing, Dede.'

As she turned to go Wigwe ground his teeth. He always did this when he felt any strong emotions whether of anger, happiness or pity. This time his feelings did not fall into any particular category, but all the same they were strong, very strong; so strong that he let fall a tear. Later Adaku joined her husband in the hall.

'How can we reward Ihuoma?' she asked.

'That's just my problem.'

'Will yams do?'

'Have we any good yams? The old yams are dry and mostly rotten, the new yams are not out yet.'

'That is true. Maybe we could offer her a part of the game Nnadi brought from Ekwe's trap yesterday.'

'That is a good idea.'

'My lord, this is of course an interim measure. We must do something really big for her when Ekwueme recovers.'

'Of course we will, but it will require some thinking out.'

Towards evening Nkechi went to fetch Ihuoma. In anticipation she had prepared an early meal and fed her children. She was playing with them when Nkechi arrived. As soon as she saw her she rose and Nkechi helped her escort the children to Nnadi's. Then they went off.

'Did he sleep well?' she asked.

'Very well indeed,' Nkechi replied. 'When he got up he asked for food and consumed an astonishing heap of foo-foo.'

'Has Anyika arrived?'

'Not before I left our compound.'

When they entered Ekwueme's room they found Anyika there already. He was mixing the antidote. This time there was no difficulty at all. Ekwueme drank the medicine without a fuss. He

188

looked much better. Indeed to anyone who was not aware of the events of the past few days he looked perfectly normal. He talked little but he did talk sense.

This time, although he was very pleased to see Ihuoma he was not as demonstrative as he was in the morning. He did not request her to sit by him. She sat by him voluntarily and they talked light-heartedly. Presently Anyika and the others left them alone.

'Ekwe, you look very well,' she said.

'I think I am.'

'Anyika's medicine is powerful.'

'You have done more than Anyika's medicine.'

Ihuoma sensed Ekwueme's old reserved nature reasserting itself. She realized in a flash that she was no longer dealing with an insane man. With that she discarded her forced bravado and feminine punctiliousness took over.

'I am sorry to have bothered you so much,' he said gravely.

'Ekwe, you know it is no bother at all.'

'It all seems unmanly and quite shameful.'

'Don't say things like that.'

'Oh yes it is, Ihuoma.'

'Is it shameful for me to be near you?'

'No, sit down, Ihuoma. Don't go away. Don't mind what I say very much. The wrong words seem to be getting into my mouth.'

'Please don't think I am annoyed.'

'I have never seen you annoyed, Ihuoma. I wish I had a mind like yours, always taking things as they come, never worrying unduly.'

Ihuoma had nothing to say, so she sat and just listened. Ekwueme talked on and on in a soft low tone. He seemed his old self again. As Ihuoma watched him, past events looked like hallucinations. Here was the old Ekwe, sensible, considerate and gentle.

'Ihuoma, we have not sat so close for a long time,' he went on.

'No.'

'My illness, or call it what you like, is almost a blessing in that respect.'

'I don't know.'

'Yes, it is.'

'If you think so.'

'I think so.'

'That is good.'

'Ihuoma.'

'Yes, Ekwe.'

'You don't mind being with me?'

'No.'

'Sure?'

'Yes.'

'Will you come tomorrow morning?'

'If you want me to.'

'I want you to.'

'All right.'

'But I shall not tell my parents to call you. They will know I am pretending this time. You see, I am well now.'

'You can send Nkechi to fetch me if you like.'

'Can't you come without her?'

'Not regularly.'

'Ihuoma, I love you even more than before.'

'I know it, Ekwe.'

'What shall I do about it?'

'Nothing.'

'Why?'

'I don't know.'

Ekwueme came closer and held her hands. She did not resist. But that was Ihuoma, always polite, never giving offence, he thought. Only one who did not know her would misinterpret her submission. Ekwueme knew her well enough and let her hands go gently.

'Perhaps you want to go now?'

'Yes, it is getting late.'

'I shall see you tomorrow.'

'All right.'

CHAPTER TWENTY-EIGHT

Ekwueme improved rapidly. He took Anyika's drugs regularly without fuss. Within four days he felt he was well enough to attend to his traps but his father dissuaded him.

'You are like a man who has miraculously escaped from a cooking-pot. You need a lot of rest,' Wigwe said.

So he stayed indoors doing odd jobs like repairing his mother's roof and mending his fishing traps in preparation for the fishing season at the Great Ponds. He did not care to stroll outside his father's compound. He was deeply ashamed of his recent misfortunes. Everyone agreed it was the love potion that caused it, but each time he thought of his behaviour up that tree and all that preceded and followed it, he hated himself. He felt that even his best friends stared at him curiously each time they met him.

After the first two days Ihuoma's presence was no longer needed to coax him into taking Anyika's drug. But she came often enough and as the days went by the bond between her and Ekwueme grew stronger. What was more, she was easily the most welcome visitor to Wigwe's compound. Wigwe and his wife grew to love her as they did their children. Often Adaku returned Ihuoma's visits and they began to do many things together. Now Adaku felt lonely on the farm path without Ihuoma's company. She persuaded Ihuoma to shift her stall so that they would be near each other at the waterside market. Adaku was not merely showing her appreciation for what Ihuoma had done for them, she was irresistibly drawn by her. Now that she knew her better, she was so disarmed that she confessed and apologized for some of the wrong opinions she once held of her.

The one place Ekwueme always went to when he did stroll out was Ihuoma's compound. He went there at the least excuse. He kept her company while cooking, while cracking kernels in the reception hall. He escorted her to her farm, mended her roof and played with her children. When he started work on his traps, Ihuoma never lacked for meat. He even brought her wild vegetables and rare fungi only to be found in the heart of the thicker forests.

Ihuoma received these attentions gracefully. She relaxed and let the gossips say what they would. At first people raised their eyebrows and whispered furtively but soon her growing intimacy with Ekwueme became a stale subject for gossip. She carried herself proudly and gracefully and a new radiant form of beauty suffused her face. With Ekwueme near her she experienced an inner peace and security that had eluded her for a long time. She encouraged him to stroll with her on occasions through the village and did much to dispel his feelings of shame and humiliation over past events. He was amazed at her boldness. Here was an Ihuoma he had never known, a new Ihuoma – confident without being brazen, self-respecting yet approachable, sweet but sensible. His respect for her grew daily until he came near to worshipping her. One day he said to her:

'Ihuoma, people say I am more often in your compound than in mine.'

'And do you listen?'

'How can I?'

'I am glad you don't.'

'I would have minded in those days.'

'So would I.'

'So we are both wiser now. And older too,' he added as an afterthought.

'Yes.'

'Nkechi saw one grey hair on my head the other day.'

'It doesn't mean anything. I have seen a baby of two with grey hairs.'

'Still, the years are passing.'

'We can't help that.'

'Certain things ought to be done now.'

'Like what?'

'Like getting married.'

Ihuoma paid closer attention to the kernels she was cracking.

'Ihuoma,' Ekwe broke the silence.

'Yes, Ekwe.'

'I want to speak to your brother-in-law.'

'Speak to him if you want to.'

'But first I need your consent.'

192

'Consent?'

'Yes, your consent to marry me,' Ekwueme said moving nearer.

'Not now.'

'Why not?'

'I should not replace Ahurole so soon.'

'I thought we had learnt to close our ears to gossips.'

'Yes, we have.'

'Well?'

'All right, Ekwe.'

The next day Ekwueme spoke to Nnadi. He had no objections provided Emenike's compound was not allowed to fall to pieces. Ekwueme's parents were eager too for the marriage. Wagbara was told to refund the bride price paid on Ahurole's behalf. He did so promptly and offered to refund even the money spent on drinks. Wigwe was touched. He said he would not take it.

'Wigwe, I am ashamed of the whole business,' Wagbara said while refunding the bride price, 'but there is nothing we can do now about it. Your son has expressed a strong desire to break off the marriage and who can blame him? But whenever you come to Omigwe do not pass by my compound with your face averted. You will always be welcome here. Marriage relationships are never completely severed.'

Okachi, Ihuoma's mother, was very happy over the proposed marriage and she said so with enthusiasm. Ogbuji her husband was more reserved about it. He was distantly related to Wagbara and he didn't think it was a very good thing for Ihuoma to replace Ahurole. Still, he thought, there was no blame on his side, and he allowed matters to take their course.

Anyika was the one person who did not approve of the marriage. He heard it for the first time when he came to round off his treatment of Ekwe. A cock had been slaughtered and he was busy cleaning the entrails when Wigwe broached the matter.

'Ekwueme will marry Ihuoma, are you aware of that?' Wigwe said. Anyika stopped his operations and turned round to stare at Wigwe.

'What are you staring at me for? Does that sound so strange?'

'No, it doesn't,' the medicine man said knitting his brow.

'But you don't seem to like it.'

'No.'

'Why?'

'I can't say off-hand but somehow the whole idea doesn't sound right.'

'You medicine men are always frightening people,' Wigwe said rather irritably.

'Only the crude and ignorant frighten people, we advise and warn.'

'What advice have you to give me now?' Wigwe asked.

'Try a divination before the marriage takes place. It may help the young people to steer out of trouble. I shall pay for the divination. You have spent enough money as it is.'

'Thank you, Anyika. When can I come?'

'Tomorrow will do.'

Later when Wigwe thought over the suggestion he realized it was not a bad idea. It was always a wise thing to attend a divination before any important project though marriage normally was hardly one of such projects. Ekwueme was not too pleased with the idea.

'Whatever Anyika may turn up with I shall marry Ihuoma,' he told his father bluntly.

'Of course you will. All he was suggesting was that we should check on malevolent spirits and render them powerless in advance.'

'All right, Dede, go ahead with it. I don't need to accompany you, do I?'

'No, Ekwe. Adaku and I will arrange everything.'

And so the next day Wigwe and his wife sat before the famous dibia. From somewhere in the dark corner which contained his bed Anyika produced two manillas and handed them over to Wigwe to fulfil his promise. Then Wigwe gave them back to the medicine man as payment. Out came the cowries.

For some time Anyika cast them this way and that. He watched them intently as they chased one another and formed cabalistic patterns on the floor. Each time Anyika sighed heavily. He seemed to be more distressed at each throw. Finally he shook his head and muttered, 'Too bad.'

'What is too bad?' Adaku asked in alarm.

'Wait a moment,' Anyika said and studied a few more throws. Then he straightened up and said sadly:

'The marriage will not work out well.'

'Why?' Wigwe asked.

'Spirits, strong spirits.'

'They are against the marriage?'

'Yes.'

'What have we done to deserve their wrath?'

'Nothing.'

Puzzled, man and wife exchanged glances. They waited for Anyika to explain himself further.

'You see, Ihuoma is a little unusual,' he began.

'Unusual?' the couple exclaimed simultaneously.

'Yes, unusual,' Anyika said nodding his head in emphasis. 'For a long time I have suspected this but I have never bothered to investigate the matter thoroughly. Now it is quite clear.'

'Come to the point, Anyika,' Wigwe said, a trifle impatiently.

'Listen,' the dibia began. 'Ihuoma belongs to the sea. When she was in the spirit world she was a wife of the Sea-King, the ruling spirit of the sea. Against the advice of her husband she sought the company of human beings and was incarnated. The Sea-King was very angry but because he loved her best of all his wives he did not destroy her immediately she was born. He decided to humour her and let her live out her normal earthly span and come back to him. However, because of his great love for her he is terribly jealous and tries to destroy any man who makes love to her.

'Ihuoma's late husband apparently died of 'lock-chest' but actually it was all the design of the Sea King. As soon as Emenike married Ihuoma his life was forfeit and nothing would have saved him.

'Madume became blind through a spitting cobra and eventually hanged himself. Many thought his death was the result of an unfortunate accident, a just reward for his "big-eye". I must say I had the same views at the time. But it is now very clear. Madume's real trouble began after he had assaulted Ihuoma while she was harvesting plantains. Added to this was the fact that he had a secret desire to make Ihuoma his lover or maybe marry her. All this was too much for the Sea-King and he himself assumed the form of a serpent and dealt with his rival.' The old couple listened to this weird tale with their mouths agape. They had nothing to say. They stared at the dibia.

'Just before Emenike died I detected some water spirits among the throng that eventually liquidated him. When Madume came to me for divination once I also stumbed on these water spirits.

195

Somehow their connection with Ihuoma eluded me. The Sea-King himself probably confused me at the time. But now that I have made a definite investigation into the matter everything is clear. Look at her,' Anyika went on, 'have you seen anyone quite so right in everything, almost perfect? I tell you only a sea-goddess – for that is precisely what she is – can be all that.' Wigwe nodded his head slowly and solemnly.

'Do you mean to say,' he said between clenched teeth, 'that this girl was never meant to get married?'

'Under the circumstances, no.'

'She was to die untouched by men?'

'Well, she could be someone's concubine. Her Sea-King husband can be persuaded to put up with that after highly involved rites. But as a wife she is completely ruled out.'

'There are few women like that in the world,' Anyika continued. 'It is death to marry them and they leave behind a harrowing string of dead husbands. They are usually beautiful, very beautiful, but dogged by their invisible husbands of the spirit world. With some spirits marriage is possible if an expert on sorcery is consulted. With the Sea-King it is impossible. He is two powerful to be fettered and when he is on the offensive he is absolutely relentless. He unleashes all the powers at his command and they are fatal.'

'Is there nothing we can do to make the marriage work?'

'Nothing.'

Beaten and quaking in every limb the unhappy parents went back home. Ekwueme was in his house, fondling Ihuoma. When he saw his parents he came out beaming. A second look at his parents sobered him.

'What is it, Dede?' he asked. Wigwe waved a shaky hand and retired into his room. Ekwueme ran after him.

'Tell me what it is.'

'I shall let you know in the evening,' the distressed father replied in a husky voice.

'Postponing it would only make me anxious. Let's have it now.' It was clear Ekwueme would brook no delay.

'Call in your mother,' Wigwe said. Adaku came in and briefly he retold his son the eerie tale of the medicine man. Ekwueme sat still and heard him out. At the end of it he was still motionless. His father touched him but he shook him off gently. At last he straightened up and said:

'Dede, I do not know whether you believe this or not. It does not matter. One thing is clear, I shall marry Ihuoma. She is a human being and if marrying a woman like her is a fatal mistake I am prepared to make it. If I am her husband for a day before my death my soul will go singing happily to the spirit world. There also I shall be prepared to dare the wrath of four hundred Sea-Kings for her sake.'

'Hush! my son, don't speak so,' Adaku pleaded, but her son was already out of earshot. He ran to his room where Ihuoma was waiting.

'You are angry, Ekwe,' she said peering anxiously into his face.

'Yes,' he said trying to force a smile on to his troubled countenance.

'What's the matter?'

'My father annoyed me.'

It was characteristic of Ihuoma not to inquire into the nature of the annoyance. She felt it was not her place to interfere in family quarrels. It was just as well she didn't try to find out because Ekwueme quickly realized that she should be kept completely ignorant of the import of Anyika's divination, at least for the present. He feared she might try to back out of their impending marriage. Ihuoma, he knew, would not be a party to a marriage where it was believed the bridegroom was doomed to die.

'Ekwe,' she said, 'you must realize your father is old now. You must not take everything he says or does to heart. It is up to you to advise him now.'

'That is true, Ihuoma. As a matter of fact I have already forgotten about it all. The first surge of anger cannot always be suppressed, but it has come and gone. By the way,' he went on changing the topic, 'we shall begin negotiations in four days' time. I have told Nnadi to get ready.'

CHAPTER TWENTY-NINE

'Adaku, what are we going to do?' Wigwe asked with his face between his hands.

'My lord, I don't know,' his wife said tearfully.

'Can we stop the marriage?'

'I fear Ekwe may grow violent again.'

'That is my fear, too.'

'He really loves Ihuoma, my lord.'

'Who doesn't?'

'And she has helped us so much.'

'More than we can recount. I really believe she contributed most to restore Ekwe to normal.'

'Very true, my lord.'

'I wish Anyika had not interfered in this matter.'

'It is strange how he volunteered a divination without fees,' Adaku said.

'He often said that if people did not pay, his spirits would not let him see clearly into the future.'

'Yes, he always said so.'

'Maybe he is wrong this time since he wouldn't let us pay.'

'We paid.'

'Yes, but with the money he gave us.'

'It makes no difference.'

'It should. After all, his spirits must have seen him handing the money over to us.'

'That is true.'

'So his divination is wrong.'

Wigwe would have liked to share his wife's encouraging opinion but somehow he couldn't bring himself to do so. He gazed steadily at the opposite wall and ground his teeth. Then he stretched his fingers one by one to relieve his nerves. Ten successive crackling sounds broke the silence.

'My lord, let us try another medicine man.'

'It is difficult to get anyone as good as Anyika.'

'I have heard of a famous dibia at Aliji.'

'I have heard about him too.'

'He may be able to help us.'

Wigwe was sceptical but it seemed the only thing to do in their dilemma. It was not easy to persuade Ekwueme to make the journey to Aliji. He told his father repeatedly that Anyika's unsolicited divination was misleading. If Ihuoma was a sea-goddess then he could very well be a sea-god himself, he argued. But religion is a deep-rooted thing and in spite of himself the medicine man's divination haunted him. No one could really argue with a dibia. They were reputed to have four eyes – two for this world and two for the other world. They saw more than met the layman's eye. Ekwueme agreed to accompany his father.

Early the next morning, with their newly sharpened matchets dangling by their sides, they made the journey to Aliji. Agwoturumbe the dibia was at home but Wigwe and his son were forced to stay for two nights at Aliji. There was not much to worry about. They had friends and distant relations there and hospitality was not lacking. Agwoturumbe himself was more than prepared to offer them food and shelter.

'I am used to it,' he said proudly, 'because my clients come from far and near.'

In essence his divination was not much different from Anyika's. In some parts there were astonishing similarities in detail. But by far the most important difference in his divination was his assertion that he could bind the Sea-King and prevent him from doing any harm.

'Are you sure you can do this?' Wigwe asked, eager to give way to the happiness that was rapidly gaining ground in his mind. Agwoturumbe laughed. Ekwueme thought it was the most reassuring laugh he had ever heard.

'Is it because Anyika told you it was impossible?' the dibia asked between his laughter. Wigwe's eyes opened wide in astonishment. How did the fellow know that they had been to Anyika and how did he know what Anyika had told them? His respect for this short dibia with a shaggy head of hair and small round belly grew.

The requisites for the sacrifice included among other bigger items a piece of white cloth, a white hen, a bright red cock, seven ripe plantains, and a brightly coloured male lizard.

'The Sea-King is a proud spirit and likes very bright colours,'

199

Agwoturumbe pointed out. 'The sacrifice will be carried out as carefully as possible. It will have to be performed in a canoe on a river or creek by midnight. Since Aliji has no big river or creek I shall have to come down to Omokachi when you have collected all the materials. When will you be ready?'

'Eight days,' Wigwe replied. 'Meanwhile can we go on with the marriage negotiations?'

'Yes, but the bride price should not be paid until the sacrifices have been offered, to be on the safe side.'

Satisfied and happy, father and son went back home and told Adaku who was triumphant:

'I told you Anyika didn't know everything,' she said.

'You were right, Omasiridiya,' Wigwe replied. This was a very fond name for his wife which he used only when he was exceptionally happy.

*

Marriage proceedings in respect of a widow were not protracted. The main thing was the payment of the bride price to the family of the deceased husband. As this could not be done until after the sacrifice, there was little else to do. Wines were tendered and drunk and gifts exchanged.

Most villagers were happy over the proposed marriage and they said so in no uncertain terms. Wakiri quipped:

'Ekwe, your illness seems to have done you a world of good. You have captured the very best woman in the village.' But there he overshot himself.

'I don't like that joke, Wakiri. Stop it,' he said. Wakiri was apologetic.

'Ekwe, you are getting very serious, I hope you will still sing after your marriage.'

Ekwueme smiled. 'Singing is my life,' he said, 'how can I stop it? What is more, my prospective wife is easily the best dancer in the village. Isn't that enough to make me sing?'

'Well, what about tonight?'

'Yes, we can have a dance.'

'Will you consult Adiele and Mmam?'

'Adiele, yes, but Mmam needs no consultations. Those crooked fingers of his are always itching for our poor drums.'

It was a successful dance. Ekwe sang with a new meaning

200

in his voice. Ihuoma danced with tears in her eyes. In the dark arena no one saw those tears and she did not bother to wipe them.

After the dance they strolled home. When they got to Ekwueme's compound he tried to lead the way inside but stopped when Ihuoma would not follow him.

'Ekwe, escort me home,' she said simply.

'But this is home.'

'I know, but I mean my compound.'

'I shall do so but come in for a while.'

'It is too late, Ekwe. I shall be with you tomorrow.'

'Ihuoma, you are a difficult woman.' Ekwueme said, laughing gently.

'I am not.'

'All right, let me escort you home.'

They reached Ihuoma's house and went in. The children were sound asleep.

'Ihuoma, do you know why we went to Aliji?'

'You said you were going to see some of your relations.'

'Yes, but that was not the main reason.'

'Really?'

'Yes. We went for a divination on our marriage.'

'But Anyika was here.'

'It was more than Anyika could cope with,' Ekwueme said and told her the whole story, omitting the part that had to do with the deaths of Madume and her husband. She listened quietly and at the end of it said:

'These things are strange and almost funny. I certainly don't feel like a daughter of the sea.'

'Of course you don't.'

'It is frightening in a way.'

'Yes, but Agwoturumbe will soon fix that.'

'I am sorry to be causing you so much trouble.' she said.

'Nonsense, I think I have caused you enough trouble to make me feel a little ashamed,' Ekwueme said with great feeling. And so they talked far into the night.

'Ihuoma, I am sleepy now.'

'So am I. It is so late.'

'Well?'

There was a pause.

'Well?' Ekwe said again, taking her hand.

'No,' she replied softly.

'Nnadi has drunk my wine.'

'True, but the bride price is still to come.'

'Do you know that the wine and kola are more important than any amount of bride price?'

'I don't know.'

'Learn from me then.'

'You are not an expert on marriage customs.'

'Your lap is warm.'

'Yours is cold,' she said laughing.

'Why is that?'

'I don't know.'

Ekwueme tickled her sides and she laughed and twisted her body this way and that.

'Look, Ekwe, you mustn't do this.'

'Why?'

'People will think I am crazy if they hear me laughing at this time of the night.'

'No, they will say you are happy.'

'But I should control my happiness.'

'Yes, that is exactly what you always try to do.'

Ekwueme tickled her sides and she laughed again.

'Are you drunk tonight?' she asked still laughing.

'I am and it was you who gave me the drink.'

'I didn't give you any palm wine.'

'You did.'

'When?'

'This evening.'

'That is not true.'

'Being with you is to be drunk.'

'Then you will be perpetually drunk when we are married and live together.'

'Ihuoma.'

'Mmm.'

'Well?'

'No.'

'You make me miserable.'

'I am sorry,' she said and put her arms around him. 'Ekwe, there is no hurry is there? Please go to bed, my husband.' The way she

said 'my husband' disarmed Ekwueme. He embraced her passion-
ately and reluctantly let her go.

'May the day break, beautiful one.'

'May the day break, my husband.'

Ekwueme left her house and went to bed.

The next morning he was up early to inspect his traps. But
before he went he moved over to Ihuoma to greet her.

'Ihuoma.'

'Ekwe.'

'You are up early.'

'Yes, I have much to do today.'

'Did you sleep well?'

'Very well.'

'I didn't sleep much myself.'

'Why?'

'I was thinking of you.'

'Well, here I am,' she said smiling. Ekwueme went into the
house and embraced her.

'You are off to your traps?'

'Yes, but I have come to see you first for good luck.'

'My mother says I have a lucky face.'

'Of course you have. Your very name means "beautiful face" or
"good luck".'

'That is true. It is surprising how little I ever think of my
name.'

'That is natural. You don't use it much do you?'

'I don't. Let me see, what is the meaning of your name?'

'It means "say and do".'

'And do you do whatever you say?'

'Yes, I do. I said I would marry you and I have as good as done
it.'

'Can't you think of any other instance?' Ihuoma said laughing.

'No, that is the best instance I can cite.' He turned round to
go.

'Wait,' she said.

'What is it?'

'I want to remove some white speck from the corner of your
eye.'

'Why bother, there is no one to admire me in the forest.'

'What about the animals?'

Laughing, Ekwueme bent his head and she removed the speck.

'Anything else?' Ekwueme asked mischievously.

'You didn't comb your hair,' said she.

'I shall be off before you fetch your comb.' He ran off with the springy steps of a happy man in his prime.

The sun was scarcely overhead when he came back with two prize animals – a porcupine and an antelope – slung behind him. Before he cut them up he ran to Ihuoma to tell her about them.

'You really have a lucky face,' he said beaming.

'I told you so,' she said.

'I have fooled you. I caught nothing. I merely wanted to hear you brag.'

'Well, you have heard it. How funny you are.'

'I caught two animals.'

'Ekwe can't you stick to one thing? I am confused.'

'Come and have a look.'

They went over to Ekwueme's house.

'Here they are,' he said.

'I told you I have a lucky face. You should see me every morning before you go off.'

'I shall not sell any part of this catch.'

'Why?'

'I shall send some to my in-laws.'

'Mother will be pleased.'

'And some to Nnadi.'

'He would be grateful although I think he has some meat in the house.'

'This will taste different coming from an in-law.'

'Ekwe, you are becoming funnier everyday.'

'Well, I like to see you laugh. Those melon seeds of yours are wonderful.'

'What melon seeds?'

'I mean your teeth.'

'O Ekwe, I am going. You've made my sides ache with laughter.'

'Wait and have your share,' he said. He cut off a huge chunk. Nkechi fetched a large cocoyam leaf and wrapped it up. Ihuoma turned to go.

'Here, take the head of the antelope.'

'That should be for you,' she said.

'I know but we shall use this for the sacrifice. Preserve the skull carefully.'

'Is there any other thing you want me to get ready for the sacrifice?'

'The other items are easy. You have eggs and ripe plantains I am sure.'

'Yes.'

'As for the lizard, your son Nwonna and his little friends will look after that with their bows and arrows. Don't tell him yet otherwise dead lizards will begin to stink all over the place.'

CHAPTER THIRTY

Agwoturumbe the dibia arrived with a great flourish. He had yellow paint round one eye and white paint round the other. He walked with a swagger which made his small round belly appear bigger than it was. He carried no knife or other weapons but everyone knew he was adequately protected. Behind him trotted a small boy carrying his medicine bag. As he passed through Omokachi old men sitting in their reception halls hailed him.

'Turumbe! Turumbe!' They shouted, 'What brings you here?'

'Same old mission, to keep devils at bay,' he beamed waving the wing of a vulture which served him for a fan. Children ran out and shouted:

'Turumbe! Turumbe!' in imitation of their parents.

When he entered Wigwe's compound people assumed it was in connection with Ekwueme's recent mental disturbance. But they wondered why Anyika was not present. Some said Wigwe had quarrelled with Anyika, others that Anyika's charges were too high, still others that Anyika could not cope with the situation. The last conjecture was quickly dismissed: a man whose body could not be cut with a sharp knife could cope with anything. Most people believed that a sharp knife aimed at Anyika would only bounce harmlessly off.

Wigwe was fully prepared for Agwoturumbe's visit. He had made a room ready for him several days in advance. According to the dibia's instructions no woman was to enter this room seven days before his occupation. Wigwe was also aware of his guest's eating habits. Cocoyams and cassava were out of the question. The great seer's favourite dish was yam foo-foo accompanied by chicken soup. To meet this specification Wigwe had collected a stack of yams and three chickens in Adaku's kitchen.

When the medicine man had made himself at home in his room Ekwueme and Ihuoma came to greet him.

'Welcome, Agwoturumbe,' Ekwueme greeted.

'Thank you, my son. Ah, this is the beautiful girl in question, I am sure,' he said, regarding Ihuoma appreciatively. 'All will be

206

well my daughter, even if I have to make a journey to the bottom of the river myself.'

The young couple exchanged glances. There was no telling what this great dibia would do and they could not help feeling excited. Here was a medicine man Anyika could not measure up to. He had not spent a night in the village yet but everyone, including the little boys, knew he was around.

By evening, clients were pouring into Wigwe's compound for divination. While they waited for their turn they sat in the reception hall chatting and discussing the merits of Agwoturumbe. It was lucky, they said, he was here. He had saved them the trouble of making the long journey to Aliji. That evening Agwoturumbe collected a tidy heap of manillas and his boy could not help thinking of the extra load he would be obliged to carry on their way home.

Early the next morning Agwoturumbe went out to collect herbs and roots. The pressure of clients was much more than he had expected and he had to replenish his rapidly diminishing stock. On his way he met Anyika who, apparently an earlier riser, was returning from the same quest.

'Ha, Anyika my friend, I am pleased to see your eyes again.'

'Turumbe, what brings you here?' Anyika countered.

'The usual thing.'

'For whom are you working?'

'You know, of course, why pretend?'

'I am sure you have worked for more than one person since you came.'

'Well, then I have come to work for the whole village.'

'Turumbe, you're a tough one.'

'So are you, my friend Anyika. By the way where can I collect "rats' ears" here? I see you have some.'

'Oh they are quite abundant here. Move up the road until you come to that Iroko tree over there. Go along the narrow track that branches off by it. "Rats' ears" grow abundantly there.'

'Thank you. What about mbelekuleku leaves?'

'Those are rare. But I have some in my house. Send your boy along.'

'I hope you won't bewitch them and render my work useless.'

'Turumbe, you know very well you can trust me. If I did that I

207

should not be punishing you but the villagers. I regard this as my village and I play fair here.'

'I shall send my boy along.'

The two men shuffled along their different ways. They had a mutual respect for each other, though each thought he was slightly the better dibia. Agwoturumbe was enjoying his immense popularity in the face of his rival. In a way he pitied Anyika but felt that the people's ovations were properly his due. What was more, it was Anyika's confessed inability to tame the Sea-King that caused his visit to Omokachi. On his part, Anyika was not unduly worried. Whatever popularity Agwoturumbe was enjoying was bound to be short-lived. He realized that sheer novelty played a big part in the villagers' reactions. The people would come flocking to him as soon as his rival had gone.

When Agwoturumbe returned to Wigwe's compound he attended to and dismissed all his clients and prepared for his major job. By now Wigwe had collected most of the items for the sacrifice apart from the brightly coloured lizard. The children could get one at any time.

'We need a boat at the river-side. Have you arranged for a boat?' the dibia asked Wigwe.

'Let me find out from my son.'

Ekwueme was called. He said he had not arranged for a boat.

'That is a serious omission,' the dibia said with some irritation. 'You will have to go to the waterside right away and get a boat ready. Now for the details of the sacrifice. Precisely at midnight we shall take off for the middle of the river. There with the white hen in one hand and the red cock in the other I shall invoke the Sea-King. You will keep perfectly quiet. When he appears you must do all you can to control your fears. He is usually terrible to behold and you are bound to be afraid. You will drop the ripe plantains, the seven eggs and the other items into the river while I plead with him. When he disappears the cock and the hen will be strangled and thrown into the river. Then we shall row back quickly to the shore never looking back. He is a dandy god and so you will all turn up in your best dresses.'

'Will I come along?' Ekwueme asked.

'Of course you will, otherwise the whole thing will fail. The only person that must on no account accompany us is your wife-to-be.'

After Anyika's explanations Ekwueme went back to his room and sat there lost in thought. Sometime later his father came round.

'When will you go to arrange for the canoe?' he asked.

'Dede. I don't like this canoe affair.'

'There is nothing wrong with it.'

'There is.'

'What is it?'

'If what Agwoturumbe and Anyika divined is true, then I think it is extremely risky for me to take part in this sacrifice on the river. As they say, the Sea-King is all out to destroy me. I know I have not married Ihuoma yet, but he must be aware I am about to. The outing on the river gives him an excellent opportunity to deal with me. Look at the facts. First, the water is his own element; second it will be very dark by midnight, and we shall be the only people on the river at that time; third I can't swim. Now suppose the boat turns over which can easily happen in the darkness, where will we be? No, I shall not step into the tiger's mouth just like that.'

Wigwe ground his teeth in perplexity and asked:

'Now what do you suggest?'

'An alternative sacrifice that does not involve boating by midnight. In fact I don't want to go boating at any time.'

'Look, Ekwe, I can't swim either. If an old man is not afraid, why should you be? Besides we shall hire an expert boatman.'

'Dede, the Sea-King is not after you, he is after me.'

'Do you want the whole sacrifice scrapped?'

'Let us ask Agwoturumbe for an alternative sacrifice.'

They went to interview the medicine man. He said:

'There is no alternative sacrifice. The Sea-King is powerful and there is only one way to bind him. As your father pointed out, we shall hire an experienced boatman who knows his way about the river. Besides I shall be there with you. That by itself should be enough consolation.'

'Can't we perform the sacrifice by the riverside?' Ekwueme asked dejectedly.

'As it is,' the dibia said, 'it is difficult enough to invoke the Sea-King at midstream. If we stay by the bank he will not budge.'

Suddenly Ekwueme felt he was fighting for his life, and a wave of desperation swept over him. All along he had tried not to believe Anyika's divination. He had been willing to dare the spirit

209

and marry Ihuoma. When Agwoturumbe divined the same thing he began to think there was something in it. He discarded his unbelief when the dibia said he could deal with the sea-spirit. He was willing to co-operate to eliminate this threat to his life. Now that the medicine man explained the details of the sacrifice the underlying fears hitherto successfully repressed came surging to the surface. He recalled Agwoturumbe's warning: the Sea-King would be terrible to behold but they were to show no fear or all would be lost. How could he show no fear in the face of his immortal and vastly more powerful rival? No, it would be far better to face death at home than to be drowned or disposed of in who knew what ways.

'I shall not take part in this sacrifice,' he said firmly.

'Ha! ha! ha!' Agwoturumbe laughed loud and long and confidently. 'Your son underrates my abilities. Listen, young man. I, Agwoturumbe, have seen things some of which I can describe only at the risk of my life. Your case is the least difficult of the many similar jobs that I have done. I have had to contend with several water and land spirits at the same time. I have journeyed to the abodes of the water spirits themselves to plead with them. What is more I can look into the future. As far as I can see we will all come back safely. More still, if by a rare chance the boat turns over, all you and your father will have to do is to hold on to Agwoturumbe and you will find yourselves by the bank safe and dry.'

Greatly reassured Ekwueme went to the riverside to arrange for the boat. Wakiri accompanied him and he could not help communicating his fears to his best friend.

'Ekwe,' Wakiri said, 'I don't think you have much to fear. I know how you feel but these medicine men are immensely powerful. Agwoturumbe is very renowned and it is not for nothing.'

'Still, I wish I could swim,' Ekwueme said sadly.

'But why should the boat capsize?'

'For many reasons. In the dark it will not be easy to see obstacles like rocks; we might panic when the Sea-King appears; the spirit himself can turn the boat over. Wakiri, don't you see?'

'Your imagination is working too hard, Ekwe.'

'Put yourself in my place. The trouble is that it is difficult to feel other people's fears. Others are as good as trees to us when it comes to feeling for them.' Wakiri was hurt but he did not reproach his friend, who was under such great strain.

It was not easy to hire a boatman and his boat. Ekwueme inspected the many applicants and chose the man who appeared the most dependable.

'You will merely row us out to midstream and back. What is your charge?'

'Five manillas,' said the boatman.

'Take two.'

'No.'

'Three.'

'No. Pay four.'

'All right, I am in a hurry; I have no time to argue.'

'My boat is here. Step right in.'

'Not now.'

'When?'

'By midnight.'

'Midnight? What can you be wanting on the river by midnight? Are you going fishing?'

'Will you go or not?' Ekwe asked irritably.

'Not for four manillas.'

'How much, then?'

'Forty manillas and nothing less.'

Ekwueme realized the fellow did not want to go even for a hundred manillas. Soon other boatmen crowded around him.

'Who is this who wants to go boating at midnight?' one stout fellow said.

'Must be a wizard or something.' They looked at Ekwueme curiously and he grew angry. But anger would not do.

'Tell me exactly why you want to go on the river at midnight and I shall go with you.' It was the stout man who spoke. Ekwueme drew him to one side out of earshot of all the rest and explained the situation to him. The man agreed for the sum of fifteen manillas. He had done several jobs like that before for twenty, he said, but because he rather liked Ekwe he was willing to go for fifteen.

'Let's see your boat,' Ekwueme said. They went along the bank and the man pointed at a big new boat.

'How many of you will be in the boat?'

'Three.'

'That is easy.'

'You must hold the boat firm when the Sea-King appears,' Ekwueme said solemnly.

'I will do that,' the man said smiling.

'Why do you smile?'

'Nothing.'

'Do tell me,' Ekwueme said with growing uneasiness, 'have I overlooked anything?'

'Nothing,' the man said, his smile broadening.

'But what is amusing you?'

'Well, you see, people often said they saw the Sea-King, but I never saw him myself. I always felt the medicine men were deceiving them.'

Ekwueme thought that over for a while.

'Maybe,' he replied, 'he appeared to them and not to you.'

'Could be,' the man said and moved away. Somehow Ekwueme liked the man's scepticism. If there was no spirit to be seen the better.

Before the sun shone directly over their heads the two friends were back. Ihuoma was waiting for Ekwueme.

'You have hired the boat?' she asked.

'Yes,' he replied.

'For how much?'

'Fifteen manillas.'

'That is a lot.'

'It is. The boatmen were mostly afraid.'

'I don't blame them.'

'Nor do I. If Agwoturumbe were not such a powerful dibia I should not undertake a thing like that.'

'Ekwe, I am sorry about all this trouble on my behalf,' she said. Ekwueme suppressed his fears and put on a more cheerful expression.

'Just tonight and then we shall be married.'

'Yes.'

'There is really nothing to fear. From what the boatman told me it is not an unusual sacrifice.'

'Perhaps it isn't. Let me fetch some food.'

Ihuoma ran into Adaku's kitchen to help get the food ready. She carried it into Ekwueme's room and they both began to eat.

'As the saying goes,' Ekwueme said, 'he who entertains a stranger entertains himself also.'

'Why do you say that?' Ihuoma asked.

'Agwoturumbe eats nothing but pounded yam and chicken soup. We are actually sharing the food prepared for him.'

'Oh, I see.'

'If he stays for four more days, there will be no chickens left in the compound.'

'When will he go?'

'Tomorrow. Then we shall really feel free, Ihuoma.'

'Yes.'

'Tomorrow seems so far away.'

'Not so far. Look the sun is going to Chiolu now.'

'Ah, that reminds me, where is Nwonna?'

'What do you want him for?'

'The lizard.'

'Ah, yes I forgot about it.'

Nkechi was sent to call Nwonna. He came rushing along with his playmates.

'Get your bows and arrows and catch me a big coloured male lizard,' Ekwueme said over his foo-foo. 'You will each get a big piece of meat as soon as you have shot one. Do you know the best way to get it?'

'We know,' the children shouted in chorus.

'Don't shoot directly,' Ekwe said. 'Shoot along the wall and the wall will direct your arrows to the lizards.'

'All right, Ekwe, how many do you want?'

'Just one.'

'One only?' Nwonna asked rather disappointed.

'One only.'

The children rushed off to the hunt.

'They love this type of thing more than anything else,' Ekwueme said smiling.

'They do, particularly my son. He is quite a good shot.'

The meal over, Ihuoma carried away the plates and came back.

'Ihuoma, we shall pay the bride price tomorrow.'

'Tomorrow? Won't you be too tired?'

'Why?'

'Have you forgotten that you will be away for most of the night because of this sacrifice?'

'That should not bother me much.'

213

'It will bother your father, though.'

'Then I shall go to Nnadi unaccompanied.'

'Whoever paid a bride price alone?'

'I shall start it.'

'Not with me.'

'With whom?'

'With your second wife,' Ihuoma said smiling.

'There will be no second wife.'

'There will be, Ekwe, otherwise people will think I am selfish.'

'I thought we had closed our ears to gossip.'

'Yes, we have.'

'So you will be my only wife.'

'That is for you to decide, my husband.'

'I have already decided, my wife.'

'You will change your mind when you tire of me.'

'You don't know what you are saying. You are equal to seven women, Ihuoma.'

'Why not twenty?' she said, with a short laugh.

'I am very serious,' Ekwueme said crossing over to sit on her lap.

'Just now you are; but remember women grow old quickly. A time may come when younger women will catch your eye.'

'It seems I can't convince you,' he said unhappily. 'Just wait and see.' He embraced her long and hard and played with her hair.

'Your hair is so long.'

'It is.'

'And so black.'

'Not blacker than yours.'

'Mine is rather brown.'

'No, it is black,' she said caressing his hair.

Ekwueme's hands went round her smooth back. He gazed at her anthill-coloured skin.

'Ihuoma, you are beautiful. You know it and yet you are not proud.'

'I am not responsible for my beauty, why should I be proud?'

'That is true.'

'Besides beauty does not always mean happiness. I have not been a very happy woman.'

'But you are now, aren't you?'

'Yes I am, my husband.'

214

'I am even happier, my wife.'

The lovers fondled each other for a while.

'Is my weight straining you?' Ekwueme asked.

'No, Ekwe, my lap is meant for you.'

For answer he embraced her again. When he raised his head he saw Agwoturumbe arranging certain things outside.

'Let me see how Turumbe is getting on with the preparations,' he said and made for the door. The arrow flying parallel with the wall just missed a big red lizard. It hit the upper part of Ekwueme's belly and he fell back across the doorway with a cry. Ihuoma rushed forward, saw the arrow and fell across his body with a gasp. She was dry-lipped and her whole body trembled violently. She could not cry, but moaned inaudibly. Nwonna, her son, who had shot the arrow at close range – barely more than the length of Ekwueme's room – dropped his bows and arrows and came forward crying in dismay. His playmates gathered round with wondering eyes. One had a big lizard in his hand. Agwoturumbe dashed to the scene closely followed by Wigwe and his wife. The dibia tried to pull out the arrow but withdrew his hand when the injured man screamed in pain, the whites of his eyes staring.

'Was the arrow barbed?' Agwoturumbe asked Nwonna.

'Yes,' he piped nervously.

'Amadioha of the skies! This is terrible! But you had caught one lizard already.'

'No, it was I who shot this one. Nwonna wanted to kill another by himself,' a little boy said, displaying the big lizard he had in one hand.

Words were useless now; time precious. Agwoturumbe and Wigwe carried Ekwueme into his room and placed him on his bamboo bed. With difficulty he emptied the room of neighbours who were pouring into Wigwe's compound in great numbers.

Outside Ihuoma lay on the ground raving. She clawed at the ground and rolled from one corner of the compound to the other. A thoughtful neighbour barricaded the mouth of a newly dug well in the compound. No one tried to hold her or stop her from crying, but they put away anything with which she might hurt herself. She slapped her thighs, she beat her chest, she raised her hands, she hopped wildly. Then she did a high jump, let her body go limp and collapsed on the ground. She tried to rise to repeat the action but strong hands restrained her.

Adaku was under similar restraint in her room. She was a stout strong woman and when those holding her relaxed somewhat she broke loose and ran out of the room with other women in pursuit. She ran towards the well and when she was a few steps from it took a leap, but the barricade across the mouth of the well defeated her. Bitterly disappointed, she cast around for an alternative but they seized on her. With incredible energy she went berserk. This time she made blindly for her son's room. Instead she bounded into the adjoining room and discovering her mistake rushed out again. Wigwe was at the door to hold her.

'Adaku,' he cried in a terrible voice, 'do you want to leave me too?'

'I shall travel together with my son,' the woman said. 'Where is he, where is he?'

A hair-raising cry rent the air as Agwoturumbe pulled out the arrow. There were pieces of flesh clinging to its barbed points. The hole in Ekwueme's belly dripped dark red blood which stained the upper part of his wrapper and the mat on which he was lying. Large beads of perspiration hung on his face and as he turned his head slowly this way and that the larger drops fell on to the mat.

The Spirit of Death was known to take away people's souls shortly after midnight. That was when Ekwueme died.

THE AFRICAN WRITERS SERIES

The book you have been reading is part of Heinemann's long-established series of African fiction. Details of some of the other titles available in this series are given below, but for a catalogue giving information on all the titles available in this series and in the Caribbean Writers Series write to:
Heinemann Educational Publishers
Halley Court, Jordan Hill, Oxford OX2 8EJ;
United States customers should write to:
Heinemann, 361 Hanover Street,
Portsmouth, NH 03801-3912, USA

ELECHI AMADI
Estrangement

Estrangement is a portrait of the aftermath of the Biafran War. Elechi Amadi is well known for his lucid, unpretentious and direct style of writing.

The Great Ponds

'Elechi Amadi's story tells of the ruinous feud between two villages in Eastern Nigeria . . . on the evidence of this second novel, he is a very clever writer indeed.' *The Spectator*

BIYI BANDELE-THOMAS
The Man Who Came in from the Back of Beyond

Maude, a strange schoolteacher, tells the tale of a man from his girlfriend's past. As the naive student Lakemf listens, a tale of incest and revenge slowly begins to unfold.

CHENJERAI HOVE
Shadows

As the war for liberation rages around them, two young Zimbabweans must decide whether they will continue to live and love in such a barren land. A telling portrait of rural life and the strictures of colonial law.

NIYI OSUNDARE
Selected Poems

This collection contains the very best of Osundare's poetry. The verse testifies to his commitment to a popular 'total poetry' – words to be listened to in conjunction with song, dance and drumming.

TIYAMBE ZELEZA
Smouldering Charcoal

Two couples live under the rule of a repressive regime, and yet their lives seem poles apart. In this compelling study of growing political awareness, we witness the beginnings of dialogue between a country's urban classes.